…He who kisses the joy as it flies,

lives in Eternity's sunrise …

— *William Blake*

To : Lyle &
Elsa With love
and
gratitude
for
your generosity

Blow Me A Kiss

Jo Vaughn Gross

Grateful

To all those who have been with me:

Thank you for your encouragement, your

friendship.

And your unfailing belief in the power of

writing and storytelling.

Together we have brought this collection to birth.

Contents

Childhood Stories 281

Afterword 339

About the Author 341

Preface

Don't ask yourself what the world needs.
Ask yourself what makes you come alive,
And, go and do that, because what
The world needs is people
Who have come alive.

— *Howard Thurman*

This collection of essays and stories is for everyone who has lived long enough to discover that the essence of life is found in what makes us come alive. And because I believe that life's completeness and richness depends on the things we share, my hope is that by reading my writings you will remember and celebrate your own stories. As we hold on to what is good—the rituals, circumstances and moments of caring that we may not value at the moment—we later recognize that these experiences are what have made us come alive.

Within these pages you will find that much of what

inspires me came from a vision of an open table to which everyone is welcome, where no strings are attached and to which no one is turned away. The image is traced back to my childhood and growing up on a family farm. Along with the wide open fields and the endless horizon, I was inspired by my parents' welcome table, where hospitality was a priority and the table was stretched to accommodate whoever came. Around that table, I was taught to welcome the stranger—the farmhands who came through at harvest time and those who worked with the animals. I also learned that no matter who came to our table— bankers or preachers or professors or doctors or lawyers, along with hired-hands and migrant workers—they were all treated equally. My parents did not realize how valuable those lessons would be for me. They encouraged me to leave the rural life and paved the way by giving me an open heart and the freedom to be free.

You will also find in my writings stories of joy and sorrow, the laughter of children, the tears of the lonely, the bliss of young lovers and the anguish of aging. Since I have organized service programs and stood with hungry children and homeless families and have been aware of those who live with broken dreams and relentless melancholy, I am also compelled to tell their stories. And beyond the feast and famine found in cultures throughout the world, I have explored the blessings of beauty and the touch of divine grace, and have known goodness and mercy and forever love. I hope you find these qualities in this collection, because all together these are the qualities that complete life and the riches that make us come alive.

Even if I had a greater gift for writing, these essays and stories would not take away the mystery of how and why things happen. The only way we will glimpse the answers and touch the purpose of life is to live it—and we each one bring our unique talents to the table. This means we taste and see, we reach out without fear, we share our lives through our stories—including those lives we carry with us—and we become our own message of love. What I want you to hear is that stories carry an authenticity of heart, mind and soul and reveal a life force that translates into action.

At times you may wonder why I look back. It is only to heighten the virtue of looking forward. The key to all my musings—and I hope to yours—is gratitude and grace. They belong together. One evokes the other.

During my childhood and college years, I was known as a soprano soloist. And akin to the quote, "A bird doesn't sing because it has an answer, it sings because it has a song," when I was younger, I needed to sing and now, in my older age, I need to write. (The quote is by Joan Walsh Anglund)

Thank you for reading this collection. You will find a great variety of people, places and circumstances. And while it is true that I want "only to show you some things I have seen and to tell you some things I have heard"—things that make me come alive—I do believe in the New Creation as it is found in you and found in me. I hope my essays and stories bear witness to this truth.

Feel The Spirit

There is a vitality, a life force, an energy
translated through you into action.
Because there is only one of you in all
time, this expression is unique. If you
block it, it will never exist.

— *Martha Graham*

Blow Me A Kiss

A bit of fragrance always clings to the hand
that gives the roses.

— *Chinese Proverb*

Dressed in wedding attire, she stood at the door of the church waiting to be ushered down the aisle. Second in line to process, I assumed she was the mother of the groom. She wore a classic pink chiffon dress and pink satin shoes. In her hand, she clutched a small purse and pinned on her shoulder was a corsage of white roses. A jeweled tiara crowned her brown hair. I thought she looked lovely, but I noticed she appeared somewhat discomposed.

My daily walk takes me by this particular church and courtyard where I observe the comings and goings of parish gatherings. On any given day, a palpable energy radiates around the church doors extending to the street. Weddings are especially delightful to watch. And, so it was that day.

To avoid interrupting the bridal party, I started to cross

the street when I noticed the lady turn her head and look out in my direction—as if for one last breath of fresh air. She caught my eye and I instinctively threw her a kiss. She raised her arm and returned the kiss, then turned and processed down the aisle.

I doubt we would recognize each other if we met again. Yet the mutuality of the moment, the give and take, stays with me. I am reminded that all acts of kindness do not have to be acknowledged: that which is offered quietly or anonymously has tremendous power.

What catches my imagination is the invitation to wonder and find solace or joy in what is before me at any given moment. I am, therefore, challenged by the cynicism of our time and aware of the following: People are hungry for uplifting stories, acts of kindness and honorable thoughts—and graciousness.

I have found this to be true for myself and I experience this quality among friends and acquaintances. Even if we are all kinder than we think we are, we are not as kind as we want to be. Some of our desire comes as a result of how we currently envision world events and our need to offer something positive, garner respect, reach higher, hold fast to what is good, embrace more integrity.

So we ask ourselves, "How do we initiate a way of seeing—akin to wisdom—whereby we create a dwelling place for thoughts to rise and be rescued from the destructive acts and tragic attitudes found in the daily news?"

Could it be that reverence for kindness, joy and peace

becomes a way of seeing and an invitation to live more fully? Could it be a posture as simple as extending love to our neighbor—perhaps blowing a kiss? Perhaps. And lest we forget, might we dare to recognize that the neighbor we are given to love is often our own wounded self.

The Swans

What do you plan to do with one
wild and precious life?

— *Mary Oliver*

Because there is always wildlife to observe and
walking paths are easy, I frequently visit the neighborhood
wildlife ponds. I revel in the open sky, and the wide
horizon and the natural beauty of the marshland and
nearby fields. While the main attraction is waterfowl and
a mix of small birds, geese and hawks, it is common to
spot deer and a variety of other creatures as well. At the
moment, the main attraction is a family or fleet of swans.
A group of swans is also defined as a bevy or a herd, but I
don't see these swans as a fleet, a bevy or a herd. This is
a family. I became acquainted with the cob, the name for
the adult male, and the pen, the name for the adult female,
about a year ago, shortly before the seven cygnets were
hatched. Since swans usually mate for life I imagined
their devotion for one another and their anticipation as
they awaited their young. Their nest was on a small island

situated on the first pond of the chain of ponds, which make up the landscape. As I approached the pond, I could see the two swans come and go, back and forth, where both the male and female took turns sitting on the nest.

I have long been attracted to this beautiful bird but never had access to watch it closely. A month passed and when I returned to the ponds the seven cygnets were hatched and the elegant parent swans were gently guiding them in the water. All summer long I went again and again and observed the swans floating, fluttering, and swimming together with the cygnets growing between visits. What I witnessed was a picture-perfect family—a symbol of pride and devotion.

The winter months came and I did not return to the ponds until spring. On the first good day, I took my walking sticks and began the hike around the island home of the swans. Much to my astonishment, I was greeted by nine large swans. The cygnets had all grown up and before my eyes was a full family of white beautiful swans. They seemed to be enjoying the water and looked like they were communicating. Suddenly they all began to fly, not high, just skirting the water, as if water skiing. They circled around in a playful manner then settled down and glided gracefully to a darker area of the pond. I was glad for the change of direction as their white feathers radiated against the dark water. They looked regal, akin to a majestic armada of sailboats, only more beautiful. They were swans, incomparable.

I began to reflect on all the cultural reasons swans are

singled out as such elegant birds, their use in poetry and music, and in religious comparisons. None of these descriptions or uses related to what I was feeling. I had come to the pond restless from a week full of obligations and lists of things to do. I seemed to be in a hurry most days, moving from one thing to another. The chaotic world events and daily news added to my uneasy spirit. I recalled a tune from the country music band *Alabama*. They offered lyrics about the pace of life that say, "I'm in a hurry to get things done. Oh, I rush and rush until life's no fun. All I really got to do is live and die. But I'm in a hurry and don't know why."

I began to walk slowly and mindfully to watch the swans. They gave me comfort and carried the message of my heart upward. They reminded me of what I love instead of what I fear—grace, beauty, joy, and companionship. And what a lift their freedom gives me, the formations they make as they tenderly glide side by side, turn and dip their long necks in the water, flutter and fly.

For me, the family of swans symbolizes the mysteries of beauty and the wonder of nature. They, too, encounter swirling currents, put up with ruddy ducks, soaring hawks, marauding pelicans, chattering blackbirds— swooping up and down—along with honking geese and motionless blue herons arrogantly crowding the shoreline. Yet the swans gracefully appear to possess equanimity— they keep their own counsel and pay no attention to all the noise around them. Not only are they a balm to my spirit, they teach me poise and a desire to be gracious. To learn they are strong and tough as well makes me cheer. The story of the man who provoked a swan and ended up with a broken leg no doubt got what he deserved. Beauty does not equate with weakness. There is nothing that gives me the impression that this family of nine swans—floating majestically—is timid or weak. They radiate absolute strength of body and spirit and they claim their beauty, celebrate their resilience and begin and end their days seemingly peaceful. They tend to these values or they will not survive—even in the gentle waters of the neighborhood ponds.

I walk away, put my hiking sticks in the car, and find myself mumbling, *"In a world of such beauty as swans circling a pond, surely I am able to attach my spirit to their gracious presence. Who knows where they will take me and what do I really want to do with my own wild and precious life?"*

Destiny And All That Happens

There is a destiny that makes us brothers
and none goes his way alone,
all that we give to the lives of others
comes back into our own.

— *Anonymous*

The town where we live does not have home mail
delivery. Residents daily come to the post office to pick
up mail and socialize. One Monday morning as I
approached the large glass entry door, I noticed a young
man in a blue industrial uniform trying to move two large
waste paper receptacles through the door. Red-faced and
strained from pushing the containers outward, one in each
hand, he was obviously frustrated at being stuck in an
awkward position—the door was not moving, nor were the
receptacles. He may have been new on the job, as I had
not noticed him there before. A line of other town folks
formed and stopped as they drew closer to the door,
waiting for clearance. They appeared unaware and gave
little attention to what was causing the delay. From my

years of pushing a wheelchair, it was clear to me that the young man needed to turn the containers around and come out backwards—preferably with one container at a time. I started to say something, and then realized he did not speak English. So, I did what anyone would do, except no one was doing it—I simply held the door open and with a bump-bump-bump helped him pull the containers out the door. The young man, noticeably relieved but chagrined, quickly moved the large receptacles out of the way—then disappeared.

I did not notice where he went, and moved on to the post office window for stamps and to my box for the mail. As I gathered the stack of weekend letters, magazines and papers in my arms, I started to fiddle with my key and, in the process, dropped my entire bundle of mail. Akin to dropping a deck of shuffled playing cards, the numerous letters and papers fanned out in every direction. I suppose I let out a groan when suddenly I saw a person on the floor chasing my scattered mail. It was the young man in the blue uniform. As I looked on rather dumb-founded, he worked quickly, stacked everything together, placed the bundle back in my arms, and said nothing, only looked at me with his sweet face, smiled and left.

Reflecting on the encounter, I am reminded of a few chosen words dating back to my first year in college. In concluding his address during freshman orientation, the president, Dr. Weeks, offered the following: "Remember," he said, "there is a destiny that makes us brothers, and none goes his way alone. All that we give to the lives of others comes back into our own."

This was the era in which "brothers" meant all of us and "little acts of kindness" was coined into the vernacular. I want to think these words still have power and that each of us, without a second thought, makes a difference in someone's life every day. Often, we reach out with no strings attached and without the intent of having the kindness returned quickly, as was my experience at the post office. There are no particular virtues needed to be kind, only awareness and empathy with willingness to engage. Yet as we give and receive tender mercies, we are often mystified at the extent to which we are affected. Perhaps the verse I heard as a college freshman, or some version of it, forever holds: there is a destiny that brings us together at particular times, and we do not go our way alone. All that for which and for whom we share and care comes back to us and all that happens is grace.

I do not know what became of the young man. Did he learn English? Did he come back to work? I do know that for a brief moment the two of us were part of that "destiny" in which we are all one.

Losing The Bookmark

Incline your ear and come to Me,
Hear, and your soul shall live.

— *Isaiah 55:3*

When faced with great loss or change we feel disoriented, as if experiencing culture shock in a strange foreign country. We lose touch with any overarching reality and our scattered minds suffer from loss of concentration. The feeling is akin to losing a bookmark in an intriguing book—one resembling our life story. How do we find our place again and pick up the story line? We don't choose to be lost, confused or altered, but we are. We are grieving. We ache. If we "grieve well," so the experts remind us, we will eventually come to the other side of our sorrow, a time in which loss or change becomes less consuming. While this may be true and emotional energy is recaptured—allowing us to invest in new interests and see beyond or around our losses—the process of reaching that point is not to be minimized. Courage is needed as we flip through our book and coach ourselves to remember to forget those pages which exhaust and are unnecessary to read again. Our mindfulness leads us to an amazing discovery: we are changed, transformed. We have passed over into a different stage of our lives, and find ourselves in a new role with renewed identity, new priorities and new relationships. Paramount to our well-being, throughout this passage, is gratitude and an attitude of living the moment, day by day. Although the narrative is altered, and the effects of change remain, we tenderly hold our book, find our place, re-engage with our story, press on, and complete the chapters.

Wait And See

Above all, trust in the slow work of God.

— *Teilhard de Chardin*

A young Jesuit asked Mother Theresa to pray for him to find clarity in regard to his future. She refused, saying she would pray instead for what he really needed, which was trust. She herself, she admitted, had never been granted clarity, only trust.

How difficult it is to find our way through ambiguity and uncertainty with no immediate solutions. How do we come to terms with our emotions when told we are to wait and see? I am reminded of the words of Pierre Teilhard de Chardin to "trust in the slow work of God." This comes from a larger work written from the trenches of World War I. Chardin was writing to his cousin who was struggling through the uncertainties of war-ravaged France. I came across the writing over forty years ago and have often handed a copy to friends and family adjusting to change or in distress. Recently, I revisited Chardin's thoughts and find the wisdom offered more penetrating than ever before.

"Above all," he advises, "trust in the slow work of God. We are quite naturally impatient in everything to reach the end without delay. We should like to skip the intermediate stages. We are impatient of being on the way to something unknown, something new. And yet it is the law of all progress that it is made by passing through some stages of instability... and that it may take a very long time. Give our Lord the benefit of believing that his hand is leading you and accept the anxiety of feeling yourself in suspense and incomplete."

"Wait and see" are difficult words to hear. Yet we hear them all the time. In childhood we wait for birthday wishes, in youth we wait for college entrance letters and exam outcomes, then job opportunities. "Am I in the right relationship?" we ask. We wait for babies to be born, for broken families to heal, to hear a life-threatening diagnosis and we ask, "How long do I have to live?" "How long will it take for the fracture to heal?" "Will the surgery be successful?" "Will the cancer come back?" "Will the medications be effective?"

Even for simple things like the cake coming out of the oven or the seeds to grow in the garden, we wait and wonder what the outcome will be.

Calamities and loss come and we work our way through each challenge, waiting to absorb new realities and understand how we move from disorientation to a new orientation. This happens to everyone.

In his study of the Psalms, Walter Brueggemann

points us to the realization that "loss and gift are held together in a powerful tension." Brueggemann suggests that in order to find the equanimity we seek as we wait and see, we must embrace untamed darkness and realize that we are not uniquely afflicted. Loss and suffering are a part of life. It is the loss of control that stumps us even if we understand that this may be a precondition for something better. Yet who wants to wait in "untamed darkness"? If God is our refuge and strength in trouble, why can't we discover green pastures and still waters while we are waiting—knowing that it may be a very long time before we see the gift that comes. The delay will not be forever and the gift may be far different from what I now desire. Does the experience of waiting deepen my desire to sort things out and allow new insight and wisdom to follow?

Through the experience of waiting, we discover the benefit of believing that God's hand is leading us toward something new. In the meantime, we accept the instability of the intermediate stage. There will be an end to the waiting—a knowing. The delay will not be forever and until that time comes we will choose life and notice tender mercies. The Spirit abides and helps us sort things out and keep our balance—maybe dance.

How Did He Do It?

The human spirit's unquenchable drive for
originality and compulsion for creating art
is the compelling force of our humanity.

— *Kilroy J. Oldster*

Recently I attended a piano recital given by the
talented young artist Ian Scarfe.   An enthusiastic
performer, Mr. Scarfe began his program with lovely
renditions of Bach, Chopin and Ravel, followed by
Ludwig van Beethoven's *Piano Sonata in E Major.* As a
soloist, Mr. Scarfe's appearances with orchestras
predominantly feature the music of Beethoven, so it was
no surprise that, with visible gusto, he pounced on the
sonata.   His hands flew across the keyboard striking
hundreds of notes on the score with a brilliant
interpretation of Beethoven's masterful music. I sat in the
front row and had a very good view of the keyboard, the
artist and the score in front of him. As Mr. Scarfe worked
his way through the sonata, I was struck by the movement
of his fingers and the number of notes that filled the pages.

I wondered how he could do it. Then, the bigger question hit me, "How was Beethoven able to do it?" How could he, with total hearing loss, compose such extraordinary music—write all those notes on the score—when he couldn't hear his own work? When I left the recital, I decided to do some new research on this musical genius. Here is a glimpse of what I found, told in my own words:

The tragic story of Beethoven's circumstances has long captivated music fans. He was born in 1770—247 years ago—and is known as "the world's most famous musical genius." He was 45 years old when he completely lost his hearing. Yet well after deafness had overtaken him, he managed to keep on working and ironically produced and introduced the world to many compositions, including what remains his most famous: *The Ninth Symphony.* At the time the symphony gave its first performance in Vienna, notes on his life tell of this poignant moment of his career: "Beethoven, a homely, shaggy–headed little figure, stood in the orchestra, eyes fixed on his score, awkwardly beating time. He was not the official conductor… he could hear nothing of the great surging music called forth by the almost illegible notes he had made. He did not sense the applause which came afterward until one of the soloists turned him around so that his eyes could take it in. The demonstration took a sudden, emotional turn as the people started shouting, beating their palms together still harder in an effort to assure the fierce-looking little man of their sympathy and appreciation."

Regarding my question of "How could he do it?" many composers and music teachers have commented on similar questions. The consensus is that before his deafness set in, Beethoven was fully capable of realizing exactly how music sounded just by seeing it on a page, and while he was doubtless far better at it than most people, it is part of a musician's training over many years of study and practice, and it was especially important in the age before recorded music and computers. There is also some evidence that Beethoven's deafness may have contributed to his increased reliance on his imagination.

For each of us, all of us, who suffer extreme hearing loss, I am assuaged to learn that Beethoven struggled with his circumstances as do we. The appreciation and accolades he received—especially over the *Ninth Symphony*—did nothing to lift the relentless melancholy that had settled over him by the time he wrote the famous composition and witnessed the performance. His letters and notebooks used to converse with family, friends and colleagues reveal that his hearing problems left him depressed and isolated from society. Yet his hearing loss and the way he coped with it in daily life has helped preserve his story forever.

Could it be that we undervalue melancholy, which is simply a fancy word for ordinary sadness? As in Beethoven's case, and perhaps in ours, could his struggle against deafness, which led to his pensive moods, have been an agent for his remarkable creativity? In other words, during those sorrowful times when we feel defeated, sad and isolated from our loss, might we accept our desolation as a tool for reflection—a sorrowful time to nurture new possibilities in which we use our creative imagination and find hope again? Do we need to *feel* sad, even sorry for ourselves, before we stop *being sad* and move on to new horizons?

In such a time as his, how Ludwig van Beethoven was able to embrace his tragic circumstances, hold on to his remarkable mind and compose his incomparable music will forever remain a mystery. In my brief search to understand how he did it, I dare to believe that we cannot dismiss the healthy aspects of his loss or ours and dwell in sadness. To do so is to battle against the struggle to be human and the power of the spirit within us.

The Old Cherry Bed

The road to holiness necessarily passes
through the world of action.

— *Dag Hammarskjold*

My son, Cort, called and said, "Mom, do you still have the old cherry bed? "Yes," I replied. "It is in storage and no doubt has a few scratches, but the wood endures and with attention will be restored." Cort replied, "If you aren't using it, I'll take it as we need a different bed." I said, "I will pick it up from storage tomorrow."

Purchased from the Amana Colonies in Iowa, the cherry bed was handmade sixty years ago. At the time of the purchase, the wood was a light honey tone and we were told if nurtured with oil regularly, cherry wood darkens. This proved to be true and over time the honey tone turned to a rich reddish brown. Later, due to relocating, and with no immediate use, the bed was placed in storage and forgotten. By the time Cort called, twenty years had passed.

Entering the musty storage room, I pulled away the

cover wrapped around the bed and immediately noticed change. The wood was dull and dry and with more small scratches than I remembered. Yet I could see the quality of the wood and the promise of renewal. After the bed was carried to our workshop, I rubbed several coats of lemon oil into the wood and watched the deep bright color return and the scratches disappear. With nurturing, the character of the cherry bed was transformed into something alive and beautiful. Inspired by the outcome, I ran to the house and began applying lemon oil to one piece of furniture after another. I imagined the wood speaking to me: *Where have you been? I thought you had forgotten me,* said one piece. *I am so dry and thirsty. Thank you for nurturing me,* said another. Then, an epiphany occurred and I heard, *Thou anointest my head with oil.* My effort to restore life to the wood inspired me. I began to think of friends and family with scratches and scarred spirits.

If I give more attention to their needs, show more empathy, offer more tenderness, might I see them differently and be given the grace to help heal and transform their wounds? Could this be what it means to "tend the holy?"

Between The Years

"Gratitude unpacks the fullness of life...
It makes sense of our past,
brings peace for today,
and creates a vision for tomorrow.

— *Melodie Beattie*

For the first time, from beginning to end, I watched the Rose Bowl Parade. I had not planned to allow time for this, as this day, January 1, 2016, stands between the years and I wanted to launch into some new projects, take a walk, write letters, start a new novel—a plethora of ideas bounced into my head as I bounced out of bed. I was ready! Or was I? I was alone for the first time—ever. I was not daunted by this new reality and only wanted to begin again: write a new page in my journal, cast new light over the year to come, radiate new energy. The past year held images akin to a string of beads strung on a necklace of change. I enjoyed recalling many positive memories and felt a shadow slide over a few others. Tenderly, I turned them all over in my mind. My heart was full of gratitude, and today I did not want to dwell on memories. It was time for a fresh start. But how and what? I needed inspiration or a sign or something to get me started. Restless, I turned on the Rose Bowl Parade and thought the distraction of watching a few floats might conjure some emotional energy.

What a surprise! The minute I heard the commentators announce the theme, "Finding Your Adventure," which grew out of a partnership between the Pasadena Tournament of Roses and the United States National Park Service, I was captivated. I was also intrigued that the Grand Marshal was documentary filmmaker Ken Burns who produced the award winning series "The National Park: America's Best Idea." Within a few minutes, I knew I was hooked. This was going to be good. Over two hours later, after watching dozens of bright floats featuring characters and settings woven with roses, carnations and other flowers, a dozen or more bands and as many horse brigades, I said, "This is more than good— this parade is magnificent." And it was. I am certain the 127th Rose Bowl Parade will go down as one of the finest.

How does something this creative and magical happen? The whole production was miraculous and staggering to comprehend. Beyond the business acumen necessary for the overall organization, this particular year unprecedented resources and technologies regarding security had to be considered. Although there were no known threats, the massive influx of people into the city, the length of the parade route and numerous venues, including float-decorating pavilions, resulted in the largest security effort ever. The numerous details of organization are one part, but enormous credit must be given to those talented few who design the floats. Their astonishing depth of imagination and creativity is incredible. What they provide, along with excellent workmanship from thousands of committed volunteers, is what makes this unique flower-drenched parade roll with such luster.

A variety of names for the floats defined the intent of the massive works of art. Here are a few: The Beauty of Adventure, Adventure Is a Journey, Seek Your Adventure, Getting There Is Half the Fun, Adventure in Real Food, Celebrating the Rain Forest. Out of 44 floats, 24 were given official honors from a variety of categories and specifications. I was intrigued with the food float as the design included realistic-looking pizza, mozzarella cheese, and grilled cheese sandwiches plus two big scoops of ice cream to make a banana split—all made out of flowers. The design chosen to win in the animation category held pink flamingos moving in an unbelievable fashion. Humorous reveling animals on several other entries made me smile. The most beautiful entry award from outside the fifty United States and sponsored by China Airlines was Venture to Majestic Taiwan—a graceful and beautiful float. Other international and cross-cultural entries included a colorful Indian Punjabi float carrying a number of Sikh-Americans surrounded by vibrant marigolds. A dramatic representation of Downton

Abbey First Adventure won the Queen's award. The massive structure of the Abbey made of walnut shells and roses was stunning. Gummy bears and lollypops were part of the noncommercial entry built by students from Cal Poly and The Tree of Life Adventure brought great applause as it carried a bride and groom, married earlier in the day. Breathtaking floats highlighting nature complete with animated butterflies, bees and bears, doves and peacocks, mock redwood trees, lavender and a variety of wild flowers brought delight to the crowd. The impressively large Disney entry featured a Star Wars theme complete with storm troopers on one end and characters from the animated hit "Frozen" on the other. It won the Extraordinaire Trophy for most spectacular float and the Kaiser Permanente entry, showing advances in health care, won the award given for excellence in creative concept and design. I cannot imagine the disquieting responsibility of the judges in making these decisions.

Horsemanship plays a significant part in the Rose Bowl Parade and is wonderful to watch. There were over a dozen entries, several from local horse farms, as well as a colorful group of riders from Mexico attired in full costume with sombreros and whirling lariat ropes. The huge Budweiser Clydesdale horses, each weighing between 1800 and 2000 pounds and up to 72 inches wide at the shoulder, were stunning as was the entry of western riders from Allen, Texas, who are committed to preserving western heritage. They were attired in authentic boots, chaps and hats and rode on gorgeous horses.

The whooping and hollering mounted unit from the U.S. Army's 1st Calvary Division from Ft. Hood, Texas, was a crowd pleaser, as were the Wells Fargo wagons. But the unit that brought the crowd to its feet with the loudest cheers were the impressive 20 or so proud riders celebrating the 100th anniversary of the National Park Service. Mounted on sleek, brown, disciplined horses and dashing in their dark green uniforms and traditional Park Service hats, the spirited faces of the men radiated a deep satisfaction for the work they represented. Their entourage included riders carrying flags followed by the impressive group of riders, followed by several mules carrying gear, food and mountain-climbing equipment. Throughout the parade entries, the theme "Parks Make Life Better" was highlighted, but no group carried the message as well as these riders. With their powerful presence, they became the message.

The dozens of bands did not disappoint. From across the nation, large and small enthusiastic high schools bands played their hearts out. Their quick marching feet and outstretched arms carrying drums and instruments brought tears to my eyes. I could only think of the effort behind getting all those young people organized. Of course, the brilliant United States Marine Band was thrilling and the flashy majorettes and pretty flag-carrying young women added color and effervescence. Cheers were lifted for the all-African-American band from Georgia and the Mira Mesa Mexican High School band from San Diego. There was also a group of Japanese students and a very colorful band from Hawaii. The commentators told inspiring stories of local booster clubs and student organizations from the small towns who marketed everything from sushi to mattresses to help finance the trip to Pasadena. The most amazing band story came out of Allen, Texas. Breaking the record number of members forming one band, which was somewhere around 300, this one high school brought 782 young people from a student body numbering 1900 students to cheer for the band. To see this stream of lively young musicians, wearing white uniforms, turn down Colorado Boulevard and overtake the parade route created an unusual spectacle. How they all stayed on the same page of music remains a mystery.

So struck by all of this, I began to muse about the talent and energy necessary to produce this phenomena. To have the parade roll along on a bright, beautiful day with few visible hitches and to the delight of hundreds of thousands of fans, some who camped out all night on sidewalks, is miraculous. There was something very American about the whole scene—at least the America I want to believe is still here. Communities pulling together to raise money so their kids can enjoy a once-in-a-lifetime experience, instruments being polished, horses being groomed, thousands of volunteers working endless hours, some sleeping with the floats until completion, the flower industry working day and night to meet deadlines, designers relentlessly focused on computers, uniforms and costumes being pressed and readied, food being prepared, business spread sheets and ledgers being scrutinized, airlines and hotels handling the crowds coming and going. A group spirit, which is such a part of our heritage, all coming together under a cloudless blue sky on this particular day between the years. Then, I thought about another float—a simple red, white and blue trailer of diverse folks singing in support of returning veterans. They called themselves the "New Direction Chorus." As they joyfully belted out "God Bless America," I wanted to sing with them. I wanted to whoop and holler like the cavalry riders, dance like the pretty girls swinging flags, run out and buy a dozen roses just to smell and enjoy. Most of all, I wanted to tell someone how proud I am of a country that can still put on such a fabulous show. Yes, the National Parks were the country's best idea and 127 years ago a few folks had another "best idea" when they imagined the Rose Bowl Parade. On this day between the years, I am inspired by watching this story unfold, and up and ready to seek new adventure, celebrate ingenuity and give thanks for the possibility of new ideas.

Onward With Love

Life is no "brief candle" to me.
It is a sort of splendid torch,
which I have got hold of for the moment;
and I want to make it burn as brightly as possible
before handing it on to the future generations.

— *George Bernard Shaw*

Is there no relief from this reality of getting older? We wonder—*Where do I go to turn aside, to get away from over-thinking my vulnerability?* What we often would like to do is to go back, go back to when we felt better, to sunlit days of family life in which we were complete with good health and energetic projects. Go back to all the happenings of our full lives before the happening of old age.

But that world no longer exists. We are cut off from that reality with only our memories to remind us of the life that once was ours. Still we keep trying, remembering, wishing, until the thought pattern is established in our brain: *This is your world now, this is what your life is like.*

Absurd as it feels at times, you might as well get used to it.

Convinced, we begin to slowly go forward into a new sense of time and relationships, including a new relationship with our loved ones who have died. We even acknowledge a new relationship with ourselves.

Our other available choice is to stand still. But we know we will turn to stone if we dare let that happen. We must keep moving and the only direction open to us is forward—forward into new ideas, adventures, and relationships in which we keep listening and learning. We choose not to be afraid of unknown territory.

Daily, I awaken to a new threshold. *What will I do? I may stand still or I may go forward. These are my choices.* I recall the seven words of Samuel Beckett: "I cannot go on, I go on." We hold on to what is good, celebrate the small things and rejoice in the moment.

Onward with love!

A Song In My Heart

All my good wishes go with you tonight…

— From "The King and I"

Ah, February! This season of red roses, hearts, and chocolates often passes me by—emotionally, that is. I glance at the valentines in the stores, and marvel at the decorated boxes of candy, but a glance is enough. And since I am given garden roses, I do not yearn for more, albeit I never weary of roses. Perhaps I have always felt loved enough that the extras were not necessary to make me happy. However, this year feels a little different as when I see young people dancing and romancing, I am bedazzled by old love songs coming to mind. At any moment I could burst out with a tune from the immortal musical *The King and I:*

> Hello, young lovers, wherever you are
> I hope your troubles are few.
> All my good wishes go with you tonight
> I've been in love like you

I want to hear the old love songs: "I'll get by as long as I have you" *or* "If I loved you like I love you." I want to dance to *Blue Skies* or sway to *Funny Valentine*. Even the fun songs sung while driving stir my memory: "We ain't got a barrel of money, maybe we're ragged and funny, but we travel along singing our song side by side."

In college, I performed in musical theater productions and one of my favorites from *Showboat* was *"We Could Make Believe."* I sang the soprano lead and imagined myself as Kathryn Grayson. And, if I have to say so myself, I sang it well. It was one of the very few times I made Phil, my future husband, jealous, as I was singing the love song to someone else.

This is the thing… when a love song gets framed in our heart, it seems to stay for a lifetime. And, lately, the songs in my heart are the old classic ones. I expect some of this can be attributed to writing my life stories, so many of which go back to the days of my youth and early life with Phil, those years when the burdens seemed lighter and we laughed and danced and fell in love.

Those were the days of dreams that eventually led us to an illustrious life. That life was good, but now I am thinking more about the simple life we lived before we assumed so much responsibility.

We met at a high school music camp and noticed each other as we performed in an informal concert. He was playing "Stardust" on his saxophone and I was singing "Because," a love song that stayed with us for over sixty years:

Because you come to me with naught save love
And hold my hand and lift mine eyes above
A wider world of hope and joy I see
Because you come to me.

We went through college together, then medical school, married, had our babies and made wonderful friends. We kept up with our music and sang alone and together in coffee houses and with friends. Phil played guitar, autoharp, dulcimer and banjo. There were health issues, frustrations, disappointments, but we felt fortunate as life was good and with a positive attitude and amazing grace we came out whole until the end. Even in death, Phil slipped away in my arms. I am not sad or melancholy; the stories I write help me appreciate—and celebrate—the life we enjoyed together. As I write, I often hear us singing, "Try to remember… when life was young and oh, so tender."

No matter how the old songs affect me or the new ones inspire, I wish to keep a song in my heart, one that makes the corners of my mouth turn up into a wistful smile. I daily ask myself, *"What is the song that I carry with me today?"*

For this Valentine's Day, I come back to:

Hello, young lovers, wherever you are.
I hope your troubles are few,
All my good wishes go with you tonight,
I've been in love like you.

Happy Valentine's Day

A Teeter-Totter

What do we live for if not to make
life less difficult for each other?

— George Eliot

In early December, close to St. Nicholas Day, our
family builds a gingerbread house. One year on the
playground surrounding the house, along with a skating
pond, a snowman and an igloo, the older grandchildren
created a "teeter-totter"—also known as a "seesaw." The
design featured a flat sugar wafer resembling a board
balanced in the center over a mound of frosting,
resembling snow, with the idea of one end going up and
the other going down. A miniature child ornament was
placed on each end—one child riding high, the other
riding low. It was easy to imagine the little figures taking
turns pushing their feet against the snow to lift their side
into the air hoping, with a little give and take that each one
would keep balanced and have a smooth ride.

Over the years, I have forgotten other details

surrounding the traditional gingerbread houses, but the memory of the little teeter-totter lingers. I recall my childhood experience of living on a farm and attending a country school where we had no access to commercial playground equipment. The teeter-totter, built by my father, was constructed from a heavy board and a barrel secured to the ground. We children loved it and rode up and down for hours on end. We also learned quickly that a smooth ride depended on watching out for one another so as not to hit the ground suddenly, or jump off at the bottom and cause our partner to fall and be injured.

While it is true, considering the danger in riding them, that most school playgrounds no longer have a teeter-totter, I say, "What a shame." While I acknowledge the liability, I regret the lessons lost from the give and take involved in riding this amazing mechanical example of a lever and a pendulum: We learned balance, fair play, how to help each other have a good ride and even how to fall off. Of greatest importance, we learned we could not ride alone.

Here And Now

Gratitude is happiness doubled by wonder.

— G.K. Chesterton

A special guest was coming and I decided to make crepes. Since I had recently moved into a retirement home, where I cook very little, I thought it would be good for me to try my hand and see if I could still create something special. Along with cream puffs, I learned the art of making crepes in a Paris culinary school over forty years ago. The only other wisdom I brought home from France was to sip a glass of wine while cooking. Although I enjoy making crepes and cream puffs, the skill I mastered is "to sip a glass of wine while cooking."

Anyway, I dug out my recipe and proceeded to organize my kitchen to make the crepes the following morning. I reached for the crepe pan, which I assumed was in the stack of pans under my sink. Wasn't it always in that stack of pans? Alas, I could not find the little round, rusty, worn pan, which I had purchased in Paris. Where was it? Granted, since my move, I seemed to look for something every day, but there was no reason for that little pet pan not to be anywhere but with the other pans. What was I going to do? Since it was 9:00 in the evening, I decided to go to bed and continue my search in the morning. At 1:00 a.m. I awakened and went back to the kitchen to look once more. Finally, I gave up and came to the conclusion that dear Oscar, who worked for us eighteen years and helped me move, decided the pan was a piece of junk and threw it out. I would go to the store in the morning and buy another one.

Fearful that I would have to pay a big price for something I use not more than three times a year and now maybe less, I went to the local French cooking store and asked to see the crepe pans. The nicest young woman greeted me and began to display all the fancy new pans and the fancy prices. I dared to express my lament and told her the story of my loss. I said, "I really loved that little pan and it was still working just fine." Quickly, she said, "Wait a minute, come with me." She led me to a counter in the back of the store and to a shelf of crepe pans. She said, "These are the original pans from France, you may find something here." She then picked up a small round steel pan and said, "This is what the chefs buy." I let out a burst of delight and said, "That's it! That's my pan!" There it was, the same pan, only shiny and new, and it cost nineteen dollars (mine cost ten dollars in Paris), not a bad price compared to the others. Anyway, I embraced the young woman and ran out of the store to my little kitchen all armed to make crepes, but still wondering if the new pan could possibly be as good as the old one. Guess what? The pan worked beautifully. I flipped out a dozen crepes in no time. They were a toasty brown, no-stick, no-mess success.

Later I reflected on the whole scenario and compared it to my current living circumstances. Here is the thing… the old pan, dear as it is, teaches me that I must leave my old life behind. I don't need to pull myself down with matters that don't matter or dredge up memories that get in the way of common sense. I will look for blessings here and now, celebrate new beginnings and welcome surprises. Some days will be easier than others, but I have decided that when a not-so-good day comes along, I will think of the rusty little pan and know that the time had come to let it go.

Monday Morning With Emerson

To look backward for a while is to refresh the eye,
To restore it, and to render it more fit for
Its prime function of looking forward.

— *Margaret Fairless Barber*

"To laugh often and much; to win the respect of intelligent people and the affection of children; to earn the appreciation of honest critics and endure the betrayal of false friends; to appreciate beauty, to find the best in others; to leave the world a bit better, whether by a healthy child, a garden patch, or a redeemed social condition; to know even one life has breathed easier because you have lived. This is to have succeeded."

I came across this quote from Emerson and thought about aging retirement communities—akin to where I and others live. How each of us at times looks back and wonders about all the years we lived and how they mattered. We enjoy telling our stories and yearn for the "good old days" when everything was easier. Yet even if we acknowledge that intentional reflection is good for the soul, we know better than to go back too often.

Yes, we laugh and we feel respected enough by the people around us. And we adore our grandchildren and welcome their affection. We don't mind the "honest critics" and we learn to forgive the betrayal of false friends. How fortunate we are to have beauty all around us. Smith Ranch Homes, where I live, is landscaped into one big garden and we notice the abundance of beauty at our fingertips. We look for the best in the faces of our community and somewhere in our past we know we have made a difference regarding a few social conditions—a charitable act, a spoken word or engaging work. And we know we have helped a few souls through hard times and offered empathy and compassion when needed. And we dare to believe that a few lives breathe more easily because we have lived.

Emerson says that if we have honored these values we have succeeded. And regardless of all the noise we hear in our culture highlighting money and politics, fear and greed, I want to believe Emerson. I choose to believe that what he says is as important today as it was in his time.

Let the trumpets sound and the drums roll. Goodness and mercy prevail.

Family Stories

And the purpose of life, after all, is to live it,
to taste experience to the utmost,
to reach out eagerly and without fear
for newer and richer experience.

— *Eleanor Roosevelt*

Kinship

There is a land of the living and a land of the dead and the bridge is love—the only survival, the only meaning.

— *Thornton Wilder*

Many years have passed since I traveled through the Dakota Plains—land of my childhood. With a powerful calm and a peace that passes understanding, the unfathomable silence of this vast unpeopled landscape of earth and sky again touches me. The decision to visit my ailing sister took on the nature of a quest. I knew before I began this particular journey that it would be my last time to see her and my last drive through the Plains. I also planned one more visit with my childhood friends. I felt a bright-sadness or perhaps a sad-gaiety or maybe both, but I was happy because this was what I needed and wanted to do, even if I knew it would be hard.

I approached the reunion as an opportunity to express my love and gratitude and to celebrate memories. Often we hear that we can't go back to yesterday because we were a different person then. While this may be true, I believe that the person I grew to be was greatly influenced by the young girl I once was—the one who admired her older sister and the one who on Saturday nights ran the streets of a small prairie town with her friends. I longed to touch them all again.

The memorable drive through the Plains, bountiful in their emptiness, prepared me. I absorbed the silence of the land, smelled the new-mown hay and gazed at the vast summer sky leading to an endless horizon. My son, Cort, was driving and as we came around a long curve, he said, "Hey, Mom, look to the right, way over there." We kept driving and I looked and soon identified a picture-perfect herd of approximately thirty buffalo. As if on eagle's wings, my soul soared to see them.

Gladine, my sister, suffers from memory loss and although the family had coached and prepared her well, they warned me that her recognition of others is unpredictable. As I entered the nursing home, I noticed her sitting at a table enjoying a sing-a-long. I walked across the room, placed my arm around her shoulders, and said, "Guess who?" Her eyes brightened and, with a look of longing, she lifted her hand to touch my face and said, "Well, I'll be darned, my little sister." With exceeding joy, we visited until her memory faded. I returned the next day and savored more time with her. Gladine was fully aware of my presence for as long as her memory allowed. As I left, she proudly straightened in her wheelchair and said, "I don't believe in saying good-bye." My throat tightened as I replied, "Neither do I." As the saying goes, "it was all that easy and all that hard." I cherish those moments with my sister and under the circumstances, what more could I ask?

The drive to visit my childhood friends took me through more familiar countryside leading to the small town near my abandoned family farm. With a warm smile, Hazel, who quickly reminded me that I was her maid of honor sixty-five years ago, welcomed me to her home and into a room filled with familiar faces. Alas, the sad reality of aging swept over me until we began to tell stories, laugh, take photos, make a video and eventually, like old times, we began to sing. Even though the deprivations of living on the Plains have taken a toll, these women know how to turn small gifts into treasures. They flourish while living and accepting who and where they are. Above all, they create a way of life that fosters community and selfless concern for one another. As I left and looked back at them smiling and waving, I was humbled to think of their practical life-sustaining wisdom.

I am forever indebted for the inspiration gained from the land, the people and the enormous horizon offered me as a child. This inspiration taught me to feel at home wherever I am and to be satisfied with what I find wherever I am—so long as I keep a sense of wonder, am free to embrace the land, marvel at the sky, and breathe in life-giving air—the miracle we all share.

I find comfort in knowing that mutual values with those from the past survive and a sense of belonging prevails as long as the bridge between us is love. These earthly bonds, old or new, deepen us, give purpose to our days and courage to move onward toward the banquet of eternity.

Under The Linden Trees

The strands are all there:
to the memory nothing is ever lost.

— *Eudora Welty*

On the boulevard in front of our old home I stood under the linden trees. When planted, the trees were six feet tall; now they stand over sixty feet. It was late October in the Dakotas, a moment of joy as I had returned for a visit. Yet on this beautiful autumn day I was overwhelmed by the colorful foliage of the majestic trees and a relentless melancholy swept over me. I pondered this season of great beauty and necessary decline and felt an acute sense of transition and vulnerability. Was it the ache of autumn?

We left our family home many years ago and I did not see the trees change from season to season. I was not there to applaud their growth, grace and strength. I wasn't there to see the golden circle of fallen leaves on the ground, soon to be covered with snow. I only imagined the trees still beautiful in their emptiness—radiant in nature's wisdom, a testimony that the beauty of living and dying go hand in hand.

Our old home, a large English Tudor surrounded by a variety of trees, was grand, gracious and full of memories. The eighty-eight-year old house built of finest stone and dark wooden beams stands at an angle on a large open lot. From the time the structure was built, the home and landscape became a signature piece of stately architecture—an object of interest for artists and photographers. I admired the stability of the stone walls and the thick wooden doors and ceiling beams. The strong building materials offered a sense of permanence. The boulevard filled with linden trees framed the elegance.

During this particular visit, friends now living there hosted a reception for us. As I spoke to each guest, I knew there would be many faces I would not see again. The visit felt like the end of a season. I wonder if I will return. Perhaps this was a necessary moment of closure—yet, what about the trees? I imagine them saying, "Please come back, we miss you."

Further reflections dance in my head: my own seasons of winter and spring come to mind. I feel a kinship with the trees. I, too, have experienced harsh blows—a stripping away. Many leaves fell when I left our family home and more continue to fall. Life with its ongoing, grieving and growing story is filled with change. How grateful I am for seasons lived in the old house, the times we danced, mourned, laughed, cried, gave birth, helped the dying, welcomed the stranger, worked, loved and celebrated. Memories teach me to stay open to growth and change, to rejoice and keep dancing, knowing there is a season and a time for everything and each season carries its own particular beauty.

Our visit ended and it was time to leave. On the way to the airport I said, "Let's drive by and see the trees one more time." The morning was dark with a misty rain. As we approached the boulevard my eyes filled with tears. The leaves were beginning to fall, the branches swayed as if to say goodbye. I rolled down the car window and waved back.

Pfefferneusse — Taste And See

One should keep his words both soft and tender,
because tomorrow he may have to eat them.

— Anonymous

Early in our marriage, I agreed to embrace Phil's German heritage and learn to make his favorite childhood food. Since my background is Welsh and Scots/Irish, the learning curve was challenging, yet fun, and Phil was delighted. I made fleischkuchle—ground meat in a dough pocket fried in deep fat, kassknochfle —cheese in a dough pocket boiled in salt water, stirrum—akin to pancake dough fried on a griddle, potato pancakes, sauerbraten and red cabbage. His favorite Christmas pastry was kruntz— sweet cinnamon dough filled with nuts and shaped into a wreath, and pfefferneusse, a small cookie rich in anise flavoring.

The small tasty anise cookie also became a favorite for our children and grandchildren and every Christmas hundreds of them were made. The family says, "It would not be Christmas without pfefferneusse." The cookies are tedious to make and many memories circle as I think of all the children and "grown-ups" who have helped stir the dough and cut and bake the delicacy. "The more the merrier," I always said, and I also welcomed the help.

The following details magnify the process: A mixture of butter, eggs, cream, molasses and flour is enhanced by generous amounts of anise oil, cinnamon and cloves. The heavy dough takes a strong arm to stir and is prepared a day or two in advance of baking, placed in a large bowl and kept cool in the refrigerator. After the counter is floured and the baking pans prepared, a large spoon is used to take the dough out of the bowl. Spoonful by spoonful, the dough is rolled by hand in a long thin cigar shape. A sharp knife (or pizza cutter) is used to slice half inch pieces off the roll, which are placed on a cookie sheet.

With the first pan out of the oven, the house takes on an aroma of anise which lingers throughout the Christmas season. Phil told me that while growing up every home and every street in his small ethnic community smelled like anise. It was the aroma of Christmas. He also said that all the young boys carried pfefferneusse in their pockets to school—as did our boys later on. Phil enjoyed taking samples to his staff and nurses as they looked forward to the aroma in the office. Samples were also given to teachers, friends and neighbors and most anyone who came to our door. We also sent them to our children and grandchildren in college. A large red tin was used to store the cookies along with a snowman cookie jar. We called the jar "Pfeffer." I like to remember the grandchildren running in, taking off the snowman's hat and reaching in the jar for a handful of pfefferneusse.

There was only one glitch in my years of keeping this tradition alive: Phil always agreed that my pfefferneusse were good and he appreciated my effort, but he admitted there was something missing from what he remembered as a boy. Year after year, he would smile at me and say, "Jo, these are great, but not quite like my mother's." I was not offended as I fully believed he was remembering his family Christmas and his mother who loved the season as much as he did. However, one year while his mother was still living, I decided enough was enough and it was time to act.

I took a batch of freshly made pfefferneusse and drove fifty miles to visit Mother Gross. I wanted her to taste them. She found no difference between mine and those she had made that afternoon. We had a good laugh as we packed up a few of hers for me and left a few of mine for her.

After seeing patients all afternoon, Phil was happy to be home that evening and immediately said, "Ah, Christmas, I love the aroma of anise and inhale it all the way down the street." I told him I had made a fresh batch of pfefferneusse if he would like to taste them. He immediately took a handful, which was his style, and crunched the small cookies in his mouth. Then he said, "These are good, Jo, but why do I always feel something is missing from what I remember of my mother's?" I had the great pleasure of saying, "H. Phil, these <u>are your</u>

mother's."

I remember the look on his face. He threw his head back and had a good laugh. He loved telling the story. He said, "When it comes to remembering favorite food, this proves that place is more powerful than taste."

My comment was "Gotcha."

The Honey Jumbo Cookie

Blessed are the flexible
for they shall not be bent out of shape

— From "Buck", a documentary film

Sorting through my Christmas cookie recipes, I came across a family classic labeled *The Honey Jumbo Cookie*. On top of the file card is written: "Grandpa Gross insists this cookie must bend not break." Immediately, my heart traveled back to the family kitchen in Phil's home where the aroma of Christmas baking filled the air and an amazing variety of cookies filled the kitchen counter. While the anise pfefferneusse are the most memorable, the honey cookie fascinates me. I recall Phil's father picking up the large doughnut-shaped cookie from Mother Gross's celebrated Christmas tray, bending the honey-colored delicacy almost in half, and with his hearty laugh exclaim, "Now, this is a well-made honey cookie." He went on to explain that he suspected the other ladies in the ethnic German community failed his test because they did not properly measure the amount of honey. According to

Grandpa, honey cookies crumbled and dried out because they were short of the main ingredient.

As I lingered over the recipe, I thought, "Assembling these ingredients resembles gathering a group of people and mixing them together to form a good committee. No matter what the proposed agenda, the desired outcome from a stirring of ideas is a good-tasting solution. Akin to a valued recipe, a seasoned committee knows the value of a good meeting. A variety of talent and personality brings a variety of ingredients to the mix and each contribution, measured carefully, is needed. The flexibility of those involved is the main ingredient in what makes a good committee.

Some committee members bring the sturdiness of flour, some the shortening (preferably oil or butter) to make the dough tender. Others bring leaven to lighten the mixture and eggs for a richer consistency. Along with salt, a touch of spice is essential, and along with the spices, the main ingredient—at least in Grandpa's cookie and in most committees—is the taste of honey. In relation to the other ingredients, the amount of honey is important because without enough, the cookie or the committee will not only lack flavor but flexibility. And, if the cookie doesn't bend, it crumbles and never makes it to the table.

There are certain steps to be honored in most recipes or committees. Seldom are the ingredients all mixed at once. And seldom do thoughts, ideas, insights and intuitions all collaborate at the same time. Ideas, as with ingredients, must be carefully sifted, measured, tested and added appropriately—preferably without haste.

At some point, the decision to stop mixing and start baking is indicated. This is a delicate point in the process as it is also the point of no return. Once the cookie is in the oven and once ideas are confidently combined and decisions offered to the larger community, the only thing left to do is trust the consequences and wait for the result. How well did we do? Does the cookie bend without breaking or does it crumble and never make it to the table?

Mother Nature Knows Best

Grant me a sense of humor, Lord,
The saving grace to see a joke,
To win some happiness from life,
And pass it on to other folk.

— An Irish Blessing

In the early seventies, artificial-snow-flocked Christmas trees were all the rage. We were living in the Dakotas with snow banks all around us and I could never understand why artificial snow was added to a beautiful indoor pine tree. All anyone had to do was to look outside and appreciate nature's magical winter wonderland. However, one particular year we agreed to go with the fad and request a flocked tree.

Phil grew up in a traditional German ethnic community and the Christmas celebration was the highlight of the year. I learned to bake the favorite family recipes—stollen, pfefferneusse, caramels, Kuntz and varieties of cookies—always with nuts. Yet nothing surpassed the selection of the Christmas tree—which was large and dominated the main room in the house.

Choosing the tree was a ritual. This particular year, as usual, Phil and I went together to the tree farm, the Saturday after Thanksgiving. He said he liked to surprise the children, but I really think he preferred to pick out the tree himself. The story of the flocked tree occurred forty years ago, and I still recall how cold we were as the thermometer read -10 degrees. I thought of not going, but Phil had time and was in good spirits. He also thought since it was early in the season we would find what we wanted easily and not be outside very long. We bundled up with extra scarves, heavy mittens, and snow boots and drove our GMC pick-up over the frozen icy roads to the tree lot.

The tree farm was familiar, as we went to the same one every year, and the owner, Hank Johnson, was a patient of Phil's. He gave us a hearty welcome and directed us to the large pine trees. I suspicioned that he had a tree in mind before we came as Phil usually chose a 9-foot blue spruce—the perfect "Tannenbaum." Hank followed us around the lot once or twice and then showed us the one he thought we would like. Phil had a good eye for the tree he wanted and I was easy—usually too cold to question. I would challenge Phil on a number of things, but never on his choice of a Christmas tree. We asked for a delivery date and requested the tree be placed on a stand and carried through our tall French doors into the living room. Later, Phil would put on the lights and the children and I would sort through the ornaments. This was the routine we followed, and this particular year was no different except that after we found the tree, Phil asked if it could be lightly flocked before being delivered. Hank said, "No, problem, Doc, everyone is asking for flocked trees this year."

The tree was scheduled for delivery on Tuesday morning of the following week. Phil would be in surgery, but I was accustomed to meeting the truck and leading the three men it took to carry the big tree around to the back patio. The tree, wrapped in plastic, was carefully lifted off the truck and after I showed them the snowy path to the rear of the house, I went back inside to open the large glass doors.

The temperature was around 8 degrees and the men moved quickly. I opened the doors and they hustled inside and laid the tree on the carpet, covered with a drop cloth. As soon as they started to take off the plastic, I let out a groan, something like, "Oh… my goodness. Is this the tree we ordered?" The men looked at me and said, "I believe so, Mrs. Gross." As I stood in horror, the men proceeded to remove the plastic and stand the tree upright. The beautiful pine tree had big globs of fake artificial snow on every branch. I imagined the tree groaning along with me. I gasped and said, "I am so sorry, but this is not what we had in mind. Please excuse me and I will call my husband and see what he wants me to do."

I seldom called the operating room while Phil was in surgery. And, if I did, it was a matter of importance. Phil was always gracious and passed some answer on to his nurses—who fortunately knew me. This time was a bit different: I asked for his surgical nurse and said, "Hello, Midge, I apologize for the interruption, but could you ask Dr. Gross if he ordered a lightly flocked tree or a heavily flocked tree?" There was no answer. Then, I heard a rumble of laughter and Phil's voice saying, "Tell Jo I will call her when I am done... but send the tree back if she doesn't like it." The story became a legend in the operating room... no doubt a one-and-only call of that kind.

I gave the delivery boys a cup of coffee with pfefferneusse, but there was no way I could accept the flocked tree. They smiled (in amusement), loaded the tree back on the truck and drove away. Phil came home later with a twinkle in his eye and said, "Let's drive out this evening and find an ordinary tree." Never again did we tamper with the wonder and beauty of Mother Nature's natural pine trees. And never again did I call the operating room regarding a Christmas tree.

The Gingerbread House

Love the moment
and the energy of that moment
will spread beyond all boundaries.

— *Corita Kent*

Five o'clock Saturday afternoon and I was still cleaning up white powdered sugar frosting. There seemed to be no end to it. After a memorable family day, I really couldn't complain as once again we had created an astonishing gingerbread house. With a flourish, the family Christmas activities had begun.

The tradition of building the house on the first Saturday of December, St. Nicholas Day, began in Heidelberg in 1962. Phil was working at the University of Heidelberg hospitals and Martha Jane was four years old—a perfect age to begin a tradition that lasted fifty-one years.

Every country has its own version of gingerbread and ginger candy, but it was the Germans who popularized the gingerbread house. Some of their inspiration came from the witches' house in the folk tale "Hansel and Gretel," and Nuremburg became the gingerbread capital of the world.

At the time we lived in Heidelberg, the art of building the "ginger house" had not caught on in our country. In Germany, however, there were at least a dozen gingerbread houses in every bakery and families clamored to buy the ingredients to make their own. Since 1963, when we returned from Heidelberg, interest in the art of building a gingerbread house has prospered in this country. Currently, it is an industry with studios for the children set up in malls during the holiday season and house parties organized to put together kits of pre-designed houses. The process is much simpler than what we did—like the difference between a box cake mix versus "made from scratch." The candies have changed as well, but the fun of making the house is still popular and a healthy activity for families. Hotels and restaurants also feature large gingerbread houses made by their pastry chefs. These are works of art quite the opposite from the hand-crafted houses made by the hands of children— beautiful in their simplicity.

In 1962, I recall the wonder of visiting the candy shops in Germany. I had never seen such a variety of colors and shapes. In fact, there was so much hand-made candy to choose from that I hardly knew where to begin or how much we would need for our project. The German bakery located on our street supplied me with the frosting and the baked dough as we did not have an oven in our modest apartment. I also spoke the language poorly and wonder to this day if that dear soul waiting on me took pity and gave me all the ingredients I needed. I know our first gingerbread house was simple as we had very little kitchen equipment with which to mix and stir, yet it was a splendid beginning and of all the gingerbread houses we have since built, I still think of that charming little house sitting in the corner of our apartment on Panoramastrasse in Heidelberg. At four years, Martha Jane, with her braids, round cheeks and big brown eyes, looked like a Hummel figurine standing beside that first gingerbread house. On the other side of the room was our quaint Christmas tree holding real burning candles.

After we moved back to Sioux Falls, South Dakota, we became even more serious about keeping the tradition. We lived in a large English Tudor home, European style, which some people thought looked like a gingerbread house. Often called "The Christmas House," it was picturesque in the snow.

By this time, I was doubling the dough from the original German recipe in order to enlarge the dimensions of the house, as we wanted to build a winter scene around it. We had the perfect space—a bay window not far from the front walk-way. In the evening, we would light the candles around the gingerbread house so the neighbors could see the scene from the street.

The dough consisted of four cups of honey, eight cups of flour, one cup of sugar, four eggs, two cups of butter and one-half cup of rose water plus "hirsh horn saltz and

potassium carbonate." I could never find the last two
ingredients, which were mostly used to preserve the
dough. I used soda and baking powder instead. The magic
ingredient was the rose water as it adds a stunning
fragrance to the dough. After the dough was mixed, I
poured the batter into three jelly-roll pans, and then let it
rest for an hour before baking ten minutes at 450 degrees.
Timing was important as we needed to work with the
baked dough while it was still warm and pliable. Phil
would measure the honey colored pieces of dough with a
ruler and place them on a wooden house frame he had
constructed. Cort and Robert were usually close beside
him, but building the frame of the house remained Phil's
contribution. I purchased nine pounds of powdered sugar
for the frosting and mixed it with a boiled Crisco and water
mixture. Each child, with their friends who came for the
event, took a small spreader and all together they applied
the frosting to the roof and ground, making snow banks
and ski runs. Candies of all varieties were added and the
tiny ceramic figurines, along with rabbits under the trees,
promoted a feeling of life to the winter scene.

As the grandchildren joined the family during our
California years, more imagination was at play and more
frosting needed. We were also being sent ornaments and
candy from our friend, Brigitte, in Munich who had lived
with us a year in Sioux Falls. She encouraged us to stay
with the original recipe and even sent the rose water and
salt peter. The search for unique candy was always a
challenge, especially in the later years when sugar became

such a "no-no" for children. Early on, the candy stores were frequent and the candies beautifully displayed. Later, we had to be satisfied with gum drops for the roof, orange slices or pretzel sticks for the fence and a variety of small pieces for the walk-ways leading to the door of the house. The children created a Santa sleigh out of large peppermint sticks and filled the sleigh with tiny packages from the doll house stores. There was a skating pond and a teeter-totter and a runway for Santa's miniature airplane along with several decorated miniature pine trees.

Since we started from scratch every year, every year the house was different. I have a lot of photos but honestly cannot tell one year from another and did a very poor job of recording the event—I was too busy making frosting. I do know that by the end of the day, I was exhausted and there was still frosting to clean up on the floor, the walls and the chairs. As the finished house was carried from the kitchen table to wherever we placed it, we all gave a sigh of relief and sometimes expressed regret for some small detail. Overnight, we often said, a miracle had occurred as Sunday morning the gingerbread house looked magnificent. We all cheered at what we found and the frosting was cleaned up.

I will forever wonder what the children remember from this particular tradition. My own never say much, but every Christmas I receive cards from a few neighborhood children who participated. They are all grown up now with their own families yet every year they mention the pleasure they felt in building the house.

Several send photos of their own handcrafted gingerbread house.

We became accustomed to having caroling groups from the local colleges and churches stop by and sing, usually standing near the gingerbread house. One group sang carols in German. The weather was predictably cold in South Dakota with snow and ice on the ground. As a treat, we would offer pfefferneusse, the traditional German anise cookie, and warm apple cider. The best part of the cookies was the aroma of anise that filled our home.

Throughout the fifty-one years, I only recall one mishap and that happened the night our chocolate retriever, Fudge, took a bite out of the side of the freshly made gingerbread house. She did not get her walk that busy day... maybe she was mad at us. With more frosting, we repaired the fracture.

As I remember the energy and imagination of the children, the frosting and the large pans of dough as well as the hours of shopping for candy and ingredients, then seeing it all come together, I wonder. I wonder what really mattered and have concluded that it was the moment—William Blake's moment to "catch the joy while it flies."

I suppose like any team sport those who were engaged left the afternoon feeling good—even if they had frosting on their face and clothes from head to toe. Do traditions like this offer stability to the ground that is always shifting beneath our family values?

I certainly hope so as I purchased a lot of powdered sugar!

The Black Cat

God will pardon me.
It's His business.

— Heinrich Heine

Our daughter, Martha Jane, was five years old when Fluffy, the Siamese cat, came to live with us. Fluffy had a beautiful champagne-colored coat with black paws, ears and eyes. We loved this kitten. My father, a savvy cattle rancher who thought all animals belonged outside, was not keen on Fluffy, especially because we had an infant son, Cort. Dad thought we were taking a terrible risk in having a cat in the house with a baby in the crib. The cat was sure to "crawl in the crib and smother the baby." We paid no attention to his scolding, and Fluffy came and went among us like one of the family.

This was in the early days of our life in Sioux Falls, South Dakota. Phil was beginning his medical practice; Martha Jane was in kindergarten. I don't recall why or how we came upon the cat at that time, but expect we felt Martha Jane needed attention since the new three-week-old baby was absorbing our energy. Anyway, we loved Fluffy and after nine months in a small apartment with two children and a cat, we moved to a convenient ranch-style home with a garden.

From day one in his practice, Phil was engaged in his work and we were beginning to feel that the many years of "schooling" and intentional preparation were paying off. We were happy. Our little family was beautiful and dear Fluffy was right in the middle of every photo and on the lap of all who welcomed her. Since Phil and I both prefer dogs, we were surprised at how much we cared for this feline creature who rode in the doll buggy and was dressed like a baby.

One Monday, to my surprise, Phil came home for lunch. He loved to come and see the family, but seldom could. Martha was in school, and by then Cort was scooting around in a jump seat. Lorraine, the Norwegian lady who worked for us on Mondays, was in the back bedroom. Phil enjoyed a quick lunch and then said, "Where's Fluffy?" I said, "Oh, I don't know, somewhere around." He left for the hospital and I went downstairs to take his shirts out of the dryer. I had put them in for seven minutes, which, I had learned, when removed, was just the right amount of moisture for ironing. This was routine for a Monday morning wash day. The dryer was an old-fashioned Bendix machine that had come with the house. There was a round window on the door and the temperature was moderate. As I approached the dryer, I looked at the window and to my horror saw the face of

Fluffy the cat. She had been spinning for seven minutes and was just cooling down when I came to take out the shirts. I grabbed for the door and Fluffy fell out and wobbled across the room, obviously very dizzy. I was horrified and picked her up, put her in a basket and ran upstairs to tell Lorraine that I had just run the cat through the dryer. Lorraine, who had fire-red hair, which I swear stood on end, let out this "oofda!"—a Norwegian expression that goes with anything near a crisis. I said, "Please watch Cort, I am taking the cat to the veterinarian and will be back as soon as possible."

I walked into Dr. Rohrer's office with Fluffy and said, "Dr. Rohrer, I just ran my cat through the dryer." I will never forget his bright blue eyes dancing. He was probably sixty-five years old and had seen everything possible that happens to animals, but I had the feeling he had never seen a cat spun from a dryer and I was convinced he wanted to laugh—maybe at me, because with my headscarf dangling and my work clothes in disarray, I was a wreck. His eyes sparkled and he said, "Well, let's have a look." He carefully examined Fluffy and said she was fine and I should "just take her home and let her rest." Of course, Phil laughed and teased me and we all gave thanks with Martha Jane that Fluffy survived her miracle ride.

A few weeks later, we noticed Fluffy acting a little strange and Phil said, "You know what, I think this cat is pregnant." Sure enough, before long, and to the children's delight, Fluffy gave birth to an all-black kitten.

Now is when the story begins: We called the cat Samantha and to this day, I believe he was the craziest cat I have ever encountered! I would find him charging through the house knocking over lamps, pulling at the drapes and bed covers, chewing the furniture, jumping on the kitchen counters and racing across the yard—totally bizarre and out of control. I said to Phil, "We must get rid of this cat." He replied, "Oh, Jo, give him time, he will settle down." I said, "No, he was damaged in that dryer and he is not going to change." When I suggested that maybe "Uncle Harvey would take him to the farm," Martha Jane would cry, then Cort would cry, not knowing what he was crying about, and Phil would soften. I could not win.

One day, my book group met at our home and Samantha jumped on Marie Breese's lap and settled in for the afternoon. Marie loved the warm, furry creature on her lap and we proceeded to discuss the book. After a while, Samantha jumped to the floor. I had gone for more tea and heard this "Oh, my goodness" come from Marie. The cat had chewed a hole the size of a fifty cent piece in her favorite Norwegian sweater. Of course, Marie was gracious, what could she say? But I was furious. Phil came home in the evening and I sat everyone around the kitchen table and said, "OK, what are we going to do about this cat?" Phil said, "Well, why don't we have him neutered, it may quiet him down." So, we did. But the cat did not change. In fact, he just kept dashing around and one day I found him helplessly squeezed by the automatic garage door which had come down on him. I actually felt a wave of compassion, but not for long. He was not stopped, back to his old tricks and ready for eight more lives. I put in another call to Dr. Rohrer who suggested we declaw the cat and remove a few of his teeth; this sounded rather cruel to me, but for a house cat he convinced me this was not uncommon. So I took Samantha back to Dr. Rohrer a few days before Easter and he said I could probably come and get him on Good Friday—but he would call.

About noon on Good Friday, Dr. Rohrer called and in a calm voice said, "Mrs. Gross, I am so sorry but your cat did not survive the surgery. I tried everything I could but we had to put him out with our deceased animals—do you want to come and get him for burial?" I said, waving my arm in celebration, "Oh, no, you take care of him. I will explain this to the family." Of course, Martha Jane cried for hours and Phil, always her source of comfort, tried to explain that it was necessary and that Samantha was happy in heaven.

Three days later, Easter Monday, Dr. Rohrer called and said, "Mrs. Gross, I don't have an explanation, but your cat was out on the refuse pile and this morning when I went out, he was alive—you can come and get him anytime!" I really wanted to say, "You've got to be kidding." But I took a deep breath and said, "Thank you, Dr. Rohrer, I know you worked hard to save him. The children will be very pleased." I hung up the phone and reached for a chair to sit down. Then I called Phil and told him to pick the cat up when he came home and to have some explanation in hand for Martha Jane. I fixed a cup of tea but had I lived in California, I am certain I would have had a glass of wine.

Ah, dear Phil. He came in with a big grin on his face and said, "Look, Martha Jane, Samantha is back." She, now six years old, looked a bit bewildered and said, "What happened, Daddy?" Phil said, "Well, you know we have just had Easter and learned how Jesus, after three days, rose from the dead. Well, this is what happened to Samantha." Martha Jane believed him and I rolled my eyes and quietly left the room.

Samantha lived with us a while longer, but one day Uncle Harvey came and said, "Let me take him, I think he is a bit dangerous around the children. I'll let him run on the farm." I had mixed feelings because, by then, the cat had so few defenses, but I had to let him go. We all settled down and enjoyed Fluffy a few more years. Fortunately, there were no more dryer episodes.

Halloween On Shady Lane

It is very important
to know the neighbor next door
and the people down the street
and the people in another race.

— *Maya Angelou*

We started the evening with apple cider and a traditional supper of black bean chili and corn bread. On top of the stretched-out table was the black tablecloth and orange soup bowls. Orange candles, paper plates with pumpkin faces, a ceramic miniature haunted house and ornamental witch dolls filled in the empty spaces. A happy jack-o'-lantern served as the centerpiece with a handful of orange tulips at each end of the table. Our children and grandchildren along with our immediate neighbors came for the supper. Even though the children were restless, at 5:15 we all sat down at the table and enjoyed the moment before the crowds descended.

Around 6:00, Shady Lane, our street out front, began to fill up and we opened the door to droves of costumed children. Shady Lane, located in Ross, California, is a destination street for Halloween. The street is blocked off and the neighbors collaborate to decorate their porches and their front lawns with lights and pumpkins and witches. Sheets of white gauze are spread on trees and steaming caldrons of vapor, made from dry ice and water, penetrate the darkness. The impression of a ghostly, spooky environment is created. Musicians are hired to play popular tunes and before the evening is over, a street dance forms.

The number of children who come is staggering. We prepared treats for five hundred and a few years we needed more. Because Shady Lane is considered a safe street with no cars and under the protection of the police, busloads of youngsters come from distances outside the area. This is an intergenerational crowd and I marveled at the creative imagination displayed throughout the parade of costumes.

The small children, with their parents, come first. They are adorable in every kind of attire from angels to witches to pirates. My favorite was the year Emily, our six-year-old granddaughter, came as Dorothy from the Wizard of Oz. In fact, of all the various designs and marvelous imaginary funny faces, I enjoyed the storybook replicas the most—such as Little Red Riding Hood, Peter Rabbit and Cinderella. Of course the boys liked to create a monster outfit with an ugly face or the latest from Star Wars. No matter, they were all amazing and the children will remember those crazy times of making a Halloween costume. I must add here that our daughter, Martha Jane, while living in Sioux Falls, South Dakota, our family home, asked me one year to help her sew eagle feathers on a sheet as she wanted to be an eagle. She was about thirteen. Since I am inept as a seamstress, her feathers kept falling off as she ran around the neighborhood. We laughed telling this story and said she was "molting." Cort, our older son, is remembered, year after year, as a cowboy or a pirate.

On Shady Lane in Ross, we all took turns standing at the front door to welcome the frolickers, but Phil, in his orange sweater, made the best impression as he chatted and guided the children toward the treats. Very often neighbors came in to visit and share the joy of being out on a beautiful October evening. Our front step (a ramp) was well lighted with pumpkins—including fourteen small ones, each with a letter to spell HAPPY HALLOWEEN and a candle inside. Robert carved them and placed them in the window box near the front door. The high festival evening full of color, laughter and good-will demanded our full attention. We regarded it as a neighborhood celebration.

Robert, our younger son, has always loved Halloween. As a young boy in Sioux Falls, we combined his November fifth birthday party with the holiday. His friends came in costume and we decorated his cakes and the table in grand style. He designed his yearly costume and a friend of mine sewed it together. One year he was a lion, another year he was a leopard but the year he was the pink panther was the best of all. Foreign students who lived with us are remembered for painting Robert's face—and he loved it all.

Unlike the balmy weather of California, the Sioux Falls children often trekked out in the snow, but we always celebrated the holiday. Robert lives in California now and has his own family. He continues to enjoy carving pumpkins and creating costumes at his design studio—including a pumpkin carving competition among the staff. He helps design the costumes for his family and still calls this his "favorite holiday."

As to treats, in Sioux Falls, I started out with 40 popcorn balls which was about the right number. On Shady Lane we dealt in quantity not quality, albeit we tried to keep the treats as healthy as possible and very often used honey sticks—the last year we were in our home on Shady Lane, we had 900 honey sticks and they were all taken.

After raising our own family and sharing in the care of our grandchildren, I can't say enough for the sheer joy received from face-to-face neighborliness. We expect these dynamics in the time of crisis, but the delight in seeing the eyes of the children flashing as they imagine themselves to be something or someone other than who they are is telling. For a few hours on this auspicious evening, we learn something essential that contradicts the world around us: We were never meant to isolate ourselves from one another. We were created for community. We were created to enjoy the faces of children, the proud look of parents, and the hand-shake of an older person. We were created to love our neighbor as ourselves.

Our sense of belonging to one another, of caring and restoring hope and edifying in meaningful ways is important to our well-being—even if it is through the face of a pumpkin on a mellow October evening.

Parenting

Open my eyes that I might see
Glimpses of truth Thou hast for me

— Psalm 119:18

Cort, our older son, was seven years old when we moved him from a private day school to a public school three blocks from our home. The school had a reputation for excellence with a cooperative administrative staff. And although we knew Cort would be missing the daily spiritual attention given by the Episcopal Day School, we felt that we could compensate at home and that he would benefit from a more realistic environment at Mark Twain Public School.

I was delighted, as he could come home for lunch, and nothing pleased me more than to see him skip down the street to a peanut butter sandwich and a bowl of home-canned peaches. It was a wonderful time of our family life.

The first September days of school went fine. Cort liked his teacher, Mrs. Bong, and he began to make new friends—many who lived on our street. Cort admitted, however, that he was apprehensive regarding the playground activity.

Seven-year-old boys usually don't walk—they run. So on Tuesday of the second week of school, I paid little attention as Cort ran in for lunch and slammed the kitchen door behind him. I noticed that his face was red and he was perspiring more than usual. But I went ahead and put the peaches and peanut butter sandwich on the table. Cort stood in the middle of the kitchen with his feet flat on the floor and his hands behind his back. He showed no interest in eating. I guessed that something was on his mind. He blurted out, "Mom, Doug Duffy has made a list of boys that he is gonna beat up and I am on the top of the list." I recall looking down at his scared face and my first reaction was to smile. Don't ask me why! But to this day I smile to think of him standing there—my precious skinny-legged wisp of a boy, in shorts, encountering the cruelty of the world for the first time.

My response was even more shocking and to this day causes me to wonder. Cort was obviously asking me, "What should I do?" I brushed it off and said, "Oh... don't worry about it, honey, go back to school. I am sure that Doug Duffy is just talking and nothing will come of it." Since Cort believed most anything that I told him, he confidently went back to school for the afternoon session.

Since I believed that after school debriefing at the kitchen table deserved prime time, I made an effort to be available—with cookies. On this particular day I was flipping through a magazine when Cort arrived at the door. He ran in and said, "Mom, you were wrong!" I looked at him and to my horror saw a black eye, a bloody lip and a scuffed cheek. He went on to say that not only Doug but Doug's friend had been involved in the scuffle. The friend had held Cort's hands behind his back while Doug did the punching. Cort's only comment was, "Well, Tom is second on the list, so 'spose he will get it tomorrow."

At that moment, I felt as if Doug Duffy had punched me. I was weak and shaking. I asked myself, *"What should I have said during that lunch break? Should I have gone immediately to the teacher and told her of the threat?"* I did not know Doug's parents and learned later that Doug was twice as big as Cort so Cort's chances of fighting back were not great.

We sat in silence nibbling at the cookies and then I asked Cort if he felt we should talk to Mrs. Bong—maybe we could help Tom. Cort agreed and we walked back to school. Mrs. Bong took action and stopped the recess warfare. She was grateful and so was Tom who became a good friend. We always said, "This was Cort's first lesson in the school of hard knocks."

This incident happened many years ago. Cort is in his fifties now and has acquired notable negotiating skills. And I don't think he has ever had another black eye. I do know that he has not forgotten the second week of third grade and recess at Mark Twain Public School. Nor have I.

Cowboy Boots and White Buck Shoes

Nothing is too common to be exalted
and nothing is so exalted that it
cannot be made common.

— *Esther de Waal*

My brother Vince looked and talked like John Wayne. Honest! Often I told him this but he laughed it off. That is, until he travelled to Tokyo and a lovely young Asian woman approached him and said, "Are you John Wayne?" After that encounter—plus a few more of the same—the likeness became something of a family joke.

Vince was four years older than I and we shared many stories from our life on the Northern Plains and the family farm. He worked a lot harder than I did—he had to—yet he always took time to help and protect me from the harsher duties regarding the animals, shoveling snow, working the fields, carrying water buckets and any number of responsibilities that fell to farm children. He also protected me from other boys. He seemed to think I could not defend myself and let it be known that anyone who tried to mess with his little sister would be in big trouble.

Vince was in college when I was in high school, yet he somehow knew about every boyfriend I ever had. The summer after my freshman year at the university, my future husband, Phil, asked if he could come and meet my family. Phil and I felt destined to be together, even though, at the time, we were very young with years of study ahead of us. Meeting the families was simply part of getting better acquainted. Phil knew I lived on a farm/ranch and in quite a different environment—160 miles northwest of his ethnic German, tightly controlled small town, located in the eastern part of South Dakota. I expect he was curious, but he never said so. By this time, he had been accepted into medical school and looked polished, serious, clean and handsome, akin to what was usually expected from a medical student in 1950. He certainly did not look like John Wayne, maybe Gregory Peck, but never a cowboy. And, he didn't look like the wonderful country boys I had grown up with. I had talked a lot about him to my brothers, so, of course, they were eager to check out this newest attraction of mine—especially Vince.

Phil drove to see me on a summer Saturday afternoon. As you might know, it was the day my brothers decided to clean the barn. There was not only a strong stench in the air, but Vince was especially covered in dirt and dust from his cowboy boots up to his cowboy hat. His boots also carried a fair amount of manure. Earlier, he had told me he was a little too busy to "meet some city slicker" but he would "try to be nice." Mother had prepared a lovely evening meal and Dad was perfectly comfortable as he had met Phil and his parents two years before at the summer music camp—where Phil's and my romance began.

Phil arrived about 3:00 in the afternoon. As expected, he looked marvelous, as if he had just showered and put on a fresh shirt. But the minute I saw his white buck shoes, I knew I would hear about it from Vince. What Vince didn't realize was that Phil was as common as clay and walked right out to the barn to say hello to him and my older brother, Bob. There was an immediate connection and, from that moment on, my brothers loved Phil and Phil loved them. In fact, during Phil's random visits, my brothers did better than I in impressing him. I always baked him a "Lady Baltimore "cake -— fashionable at the time—with white sticky frosting. And, I was sure to give him the cake to eat on the drive home. After we were married, he confessed that he did not like white cake and showed me the exact railroad crossing—about twenty miles from the farm—where he threw out the cake. I learned to make angel food cake, which he loved, and while he was young he continued to wear white buck shoes. My brothers never mentioned them.

After years of medical training and with two children, we enjoyed living and working in Sioux Falls, South Dakota. Vince and his family lived about three hours away. Shortly after the birth of our third child in 1970 and shortly after Phil began his work with the total hip replacement, he became ill and was admitted to the Mayo

Clinic. Because he was one of the first orthopedic surgeons in the country to do the hip procedure, I knew he was under heavy pressure and was working far too hard. I also knew he was very good at what he did and there was no way of stopping him from the many surgeries he felt compelled to perform in order to perfect the procedure for those learning the hip replacement. The diagnosis was advanced multiple sclerosis. He was put under heavy steroids and kept in the hospital six weeks. During that time, dozens of friends drove many miles to offer support, including several "preachers"—as Phil called the clergy. He appreciated all the prayers and comforting words, but said, "If I hear Romans 8 one more time, I think I will say "enough." (This is the scripture that says, "All things work together for good to those who love God.") This is not to say that Phil did not believe in this text—he was just tired of hearing it repeated so many times.

One afternoon, we were alone in his hospital room. I was sitting in a chair reading and Phil was dozing off and on in the hospital bed. We heard a tap on the door and in walked Vince. His face was dusty and his arms full of grease. He said he had had "engine trouble" with his truck and fixed it on the highway. He wore his boots and cowboy hat and, yes, he looked like John Wayne. As he walked in the room and toward the white pristine bed, he looked over at me and then at Phil—his face flushed and he started to cry. Finally he blurted out, "Dammit, Phil, this is the sh--s!" Phil started to laugh and then cry. I watched Vince drop to his knees, throw off his hat, reach down and put his arms around Phil—who in turn reached out for Vince. For what seemed like a long time, they held on to each other. Then, I heard Phil say, "You rascal, Vince, this is the best pastoral care I have had in five weeks."

As I sat there quietly listening, my mind swept back to the barn where they had met, Vince in his cowboy boots, Phil in his white buck shoes. I remembered the fresh hay replacing the piles of manure, the cows in their stanchions waiting to be milked, the cats running up and down the ladder to the haymow, the barn doves cooing and the chickens scattering as we walked away from the barn toward the house. I felt the warmth of the summer sun and the warmth of young love and friendship developing. I came out of my musings, and breathed a prayer of gratitude. If joy is feeling good about something good, I knew in the midst of sadness, I was a part of something good.

Rescuing Joy From Heartbreak

If we can't laugh,
we can't properly be serious

— *Philip Simmons*

During the last twenty years of his life, Phil often fell. Given the presumptive diagnosis of chronic progressive multiple sclerosis when he was thirty years old and in his last year of orthopedic residency, he always felt fortunate to manage his illness throughout his thirty-year medical career until he chose early retirement, at age sixty. Because we both wanted to take classes at Berkeley, study, enjoy better weather and be near our children, we moved from our home in the Dakotas to Marin County in 1989. After a few years of academic pursuit, Phil decided to back away from his involvement in medical ethics—national advisory boards, etc.—and organize a woodworking shop. For the next twenty-five years, as his health diminished, he enjoyed several hours every day pursuing his reverence for wood while creating lovely art pieces. Known as a skilled surgeon, he had published many articles in various orthopedic journals regarding his work with total joint replacements. However, at the end of his life he said the article that pleased him the most was the one published in the *Woodworker's Journal* detailing his experience as a person with a disability who found refuge in a woodworking shop creating dovetail joints. He worked from his wheelchair or transferred to a high stool and, fortunately, had the use of his upper extremities. I believe it was during those quiet, peaceful hours in his shop that Phil came to terms with his disability. It was there that he explored the narrow reality of rescuing joy from heartbreak.

Now that I am alone and find myself becoming more earnest about my own disabilities, I try to remember his example. I also remember the times we laughed and turned to humor for the obvious reasons of distraction and relief. Through our sixty years together, we kept an agreement that if we couldn't laugh, we couldn't properly be serious—and we laughed a lot at ourselves and our circumstances. In my own search for peace since his death, I claim some health benefit when I think of the following stories—most of which came as a result of his falling down. These stories are a mere sample of living with a disability, and to remember how we laughed together helps me as I pursue the seriousness of my own difficulties and, during the process, look for amusement.

The majority of Phil's falls occurred in the bathroom and bedroom or on his way to and from the shop. With the use of grab bars, he was able to move around the bathroom but every so often he missed the bar when he swung his arm for the grab and fell. At first, I would try and figure out how to lift him up. He would struggle and I would try everything imaginable from rugs to towels, but eventually gave it up and started calling the paramedics. What a splendid group of young men! They came often and soon became our friends. One day one of the men asked Phil, "How do you manage to get around in here [meaning the bathroom]?" Phil said, "I just swing from bar to bar." With a twinkle in his eye, the young man replied, "Oh… well, we have a man we pick up every Saturday night who swings from bar to bar." After a number of calls, I asked the men if I should prepare tea next time! They were a jolly team and we all worked together to help Phil. When I saw them "around town" in the grocery stores or on the street, they would come up and kiss me on the forehead or give me a hug. I loved those guys! They never made me feel I was asking too much and they always left us smiling.

Another incident happened in a resort hotel, far away from the paramedics. Phil was stronger then—meaning he was still able to walk with a walker. A few hours after we had gone to bed, he called and said, "Jo, would you help me, I'm on the floor, I fell out of bed." I was half asleep and said, "What? It's 1:00 in the morning!" He replied, "I know it's 1:00 in the morning, but I am on the floor and can't get up." I said, "Oh, that's too bad, just a minute." I was still groggy but stirred out of bed, walked around to his side and as I looked down, stumbled over my long white nightgown and fell right on top of him. He said, "Well, you woke up." I said, "What do we do now?" He said, "I suggest you get two pillows and a blanket and we will spend the night on the floor." Then, we laughed. In fact, we laughed every time we thought of that scenario. I can't recall how we recovered. I think we managed to reach for the bed or something and Phil was upright again. I know we were still managing alone.

The short distance from the kitchen door to the shop door was a bit precarious. We built a ramp and Phil was, for the most part, independent on his walker or in the wheelchair. I was always a bit anxious that he would lose control of his motorized chair and end up in the swimming pool, which was close to the house. Fortunately, that never happened, but one day I came out to the patio and found him in the mint patch, which grew in abundance near his shop. He was trying to use his walker and lost control of his body and fell face down among the mint. When I saw him, I cried, "What happened?" He said, "How about a mint julep?" For weeks, he smelled like mint. The fragrance was in his ears, nose, hair, and clothing and even in his shoes. I remember the grandchildren teasing him and the laughter—always the laughter.

And then there was the story of the last day he drove the car. This was earlier than the above stories, before the walker and wheelchair, only the cane. Still driving, he had driven home from church, dropped me off at the front door and driven on toward the garage to put the car away. His foot slipped and he ran into the side of the garage. I had gone into the kitchen and thought we were having an earthquake as there was a loud rumble from the impact. I ran out to find him unhurt but with a bizarre scene of the car crashed against the garage door. There was nothing major to be repaired, but Phil was deeply disturbed. I had never seen him so defeated.

What is memorable, and for what I am to this day ashamed of, is that I viewed it as being very funny—akin to a Steve Martin movie. I helped him to a chair on the patio and ran into the house as I had uncontrollable laughter and did not want him to know how amusing it all seemed. Every few minutes I would go back out with ice water or coffee and try to cheer him up. Then my daughter, Martha, and son-in-law, Joseph, came and found the car at its crazy angle. Martha, who knew I had driven from Stanford the day before to see our son, Robert, said, "Mom, did you drink too much wine last night?" She also started to laugh so we both ran in the house and laughed together. Dear Phil still could not find anything funny about what happened. Joseph stayed with him and Phil admitted to him that his driving days were over. Martha and I were trying to behave and finally calmed down. We carried our lunch out to the picnic table and talked about other things, but Phil was still very quiet. Joseph said he, Joseph, needed a nap and went to the cabana near the pool, behind the garage, and slept on a daybed for about twenty minutes. When he got up, he came to the picnic table and said, "H. Phil, I just had the best nap, I think it was the cross ventilation you created in the garage." Joe had struck the right chord. Phil started to laugh with us and with a glass of wine we convinced him that there was no serious damage. However, on that particular day, we made the decision to turn the garage into a woodworking shop.

As the saying goes, "The rest is history." The shop became a life-giving refuge. Phil cherished his hours there and for twenty-five years created wooden art pieces. He made Christmas and birthday presents, crosses for the church officers, and lovely trays, bowls and vases. His reverence for wood led to his search for unusual varieties—allowing him to create pieces of unusual beauty.

Joy from heartbreak is not always easy to rescue. Phil found a way. And for those of us who loved him and watched him struggle and learn to fall, we say, "Bravo and thank you for your resilience." As for the laughter, perhaps it was to cover up our own heartache. I know since Phil is gone and I find myself getting unbearably earnest, I try to remember how we laughed.

Letting Go Of The Land

We had left no mark on the country itself,
But the land had left its mark on us."

— *Sigurd Olson*

*Phil and I wrote the following story together and tell
it in his voice. The experience was cathartic as we both
loved the farm and remain ever grateful for all that
happened there.*

She looked out toward the rose garden near the back
door of our Ross, California, home and quietly said, "Phil,
I believe the time has come to sell the farm, what do you
think?" For a moment, I didn't think or feel, I quaked. Jo
repeated the question only this time added, "It takes more
energy each summer to make the trip back to South Dakota
and neither of us is able to do the things we used to do.
Remember the last time we tried to wheel the garbage can
to the road for pick-up? We ended up falling on top of
each other." "Yes," I mumbled, "Yes, I remember how

we laughed." We laughed again, and then quieted. Although we had spoken in generalities before about letting go of the land, we usually dropped the subject. After twenty-seven years of loving the farm, we found it too difficult to think about leaving it. Finally, a voice deep within me said, *"I know the time has come. I've known it for some time and we need to make it happen sooner than later."* Yet, I felt numb and said to myself, *"I can't imagine life without the farm."*

After Jo left for her morning errands, I called our realtor, an old friend in Sioux Falls, who was well acquainted with the property. He said, "Phil, you love that place, are you sure you want to do this?" I said, "Yes, Mick, the time has come." The call was made in the spring of 1998 and the process of selling began.

The history of our acquiring the land began on a Saturday afternoon in September, 1971. While I was attending a medical conference, Don, an old school friend of Jo's, stopped by to say hello. When Jo asked him what he was doing now, he said, "I am in real estate and sell farms." Jo expressed her interest in finding a small farm. She explained that I was given the diagnosis of multiple sclerosis and was desirous of finding land where I could have a vegetable garden and be outdoors. Don said, "What are you doing this afternoon?" Jo went with him and without hesitation told Don that she wanted to purchase the fifty-five acre farm. Jo was confident that she had found the right place for us to rest and relax. She was excited for me to explore the grounds and the following weekend we drove out to see the property. I quickly engaged with her vision for what might be and we started the process of acquiring the land.

Located thirty-five miles north of Sioux Falls near the Sioux River and the small town of Egan, the farm grounds radiated a calm, welcoming effect—mellow and peaceful. At the time, I admitted that my orthopedic practice consumed me. I had recently introduced the total hip replacement to the area and was immersed in teaching and developing the technique. Along with the diagnosis, Jo recognized my need to get out of the operating room and into the fresh air. This was her answer. The farm was a great idea and I immediately took to the possibilities it offered. We called the small acreage Comaro Meadows— after our three children: Cort, Martha and Robert. .

The following twenty-seven years we nurtured, agonized over, and loved our experience on the land. Little did Jo know I would attack the farm project with the same enthusiasm as my medical practice. I was always extending myself too far; raising too much of this or that, taxing all concerned. We grew Hereford cattle, feeder pigs, ducks, geese, capon chicken, rabbits, pheasants, and riding horses. Each spring I planted 3000 gladiola bulbs only to lift them in the fall and repeat the process all over again the next year. If Burpee Seeds promoted a new tomato seed, I had to try it. The vegetable garden was immense and the yields profuse—especially tomatoes. Jo would say, "Bring me a few tomatoes for lunch." I would walk in with two bushels. She would look at me and scream, "What do you think I am going to do with all those tomatoes?" Then she would start preserving. We recall having dozens of jars filled with green beans, tomatoes, carrots, and pickles in the pantry. Jo would preserve them in the farm kitchen, then carry them to the basement of our Sioux Falls home. We also had chickens, ducks, and a side of beef in the freezer. We were trying to act like self-sustaining farmers.

While all this work was going on, we also hosted family and friends and numerous guests from near and far. Hospitality is a rule of our household and since Jo enjoyed cooking in the farm kitchen, we have fond memories of homemade bread, ice cream, apple and strawberry pies plus fresh vegetables from the garden and barbeques with fresh sweet corn. We had fun inviting friends from town for a corn-picking evening. The idea was to start the water boiling on the stove and then go to the garden and harvest the corn on the cob. We quickly pulled off the husks and dropped the corn in the boiling water. After a few minutes, we pulled the corn out of the water and smothered the ears with butter. There was never better corn—or a better party.

In addition to family and local friends, we enjoyed foreign families and friends from distant large cities—people unfamiliar with farming and rural life. One summer Krishna, a friend from Nepal and a white-water rafter on the gigantic Himalayan rivers, took Robert, age fourteen, and his friend, Mark, down the Sioux River in a canoe. The river ran through our property. When we said the muddy Sioux could never be as exciting as the turbulent Dude Khosi, Krishna said he had never been on a river that was not exciting. To which Mark replied, "I guess he's never been on the Sioux." But we loved the Sioux River, in spite of the problems of living beside a river that ran wild. When the boys were young, we built rafts, went fishing and had a small paddle boat. Our older son, Cort, fantasized that he was Huckleberry Finn and spent hours on the river.

The farm house challenged our imagination for years of remodeling. What started as a hundred-year-old simple house—more like a shack—with two small bedrooms, an antique bathroom and kitchen and a lean-to porch grew to a ranch-style home with outside decks, a large kitchen, fireplace, sun porch, four bedrooms and four baths.

We also expanded from fifty-five to five hundred fifty acres of crop land. An irrigation system was developed, along with large storage bins to preserve the grain for later use. I invested in tractors, pickup trucks, mowers, tools and garden equipment. We planted trees, landscaped the yard, built fences, installed outdoor lighting, and hired men to help with the upkeep. When I wasn't on call or traveling, I drove out every Thursday and many weekends throughout the year. When the children were young, Jo stayed most of the summers. I never took call at the farm, but drove back and forth to the hospitals. It became a way of life—I loved it.

When my multiple sclerosis took a turn for the worse in 1988, I retired from my medical practice and within a year we decided to move to the San Francisco Bay area near our children. Two of them were out of college, married and living in San Francisco. Robert was enrolled at Stanford. We sold the family home in Sioux Falls and kept the farm. Our plan was to return in the summers—stay at the farm—and see our relatives and friends. After nine years and five grandchildren wondering where we were in the summertime, we realized the dream was impractical. South Dakota was too far away for us to care for or enjoy the experience we once knew and too far away and complicated for the children to maintain. With great reluctance, the process of letting go began.

First, the added land was sold in parcels to neighbors who had been farming it over the years. Soon we were down to the original fifty-five acres and the greatly enhanced farm house. The animals sold quickly. The farm was listed with a broker and we pondered what to do with the contents of the farm house and the barns. The best resolution seemed to have an auction sale. We were faced with an accumulation of furniture, dishes, fruit jars, cookware, paintings, and linens plus family memorabilia collected and stored in the farm house attic. The barns were full of tractors, boats, horse tack, wire, fence posts, garden pots, tillers, rubber hoses, spades, pitchforks, saws and shovels. There was a 1989 black Cadillac, an antique sleigh and buggy plus a playhouse full of toys. All of these items needed to be sorted through for auction.

Jo and I spent two weeks in South Dakota getting ready for the sale. The first week a semi-trailer bound for

California was loaded with furniture and sundry items for the families. While this was happening, we were wise enough to stay at a hotel in Sioux Falls and drive out to "work" every morning. Separation from the task a few hours every day helped relieve the emotional burden of the final closure. Old friends gathered around us in the evenings, offering concern, comfort and joy.

The drive both to and from the farm during those mid-September days of 1998 is memorable. We left the hotel as the sun was rising and returned as it dropped from the open sky. The autumn season in South Dakota is beautiful and the colors of the soy bean and corn fields, turning a brilliant yellow to orange to terra cotta, are breath-taking. We took the back roads and immersed ourselves in the beauty of the countryside. The late harvest was getting underway and farmers were working with large combines in the fields—providing us with lasting images.

The land has always been particularly dear to us. Jo was born and raised on a farm and I grew up on a large acreage in a small town where we had abundant gardens and an apple orchard. We both understood the town and country culture. And during those final days as I observed Dan, our beloved caretaker, digging the last of the potatoes in the garden, I was aware again of how much I loved to touch the soil. As the potatoes were lifted from the ground, the clumps of rich black dirt clinging tenaciously to their skins had to be brushed off. This black, sandy, river bottom loam was just as fertile as the first day we settled there. We had made a real effort to put as much

into the land as we took out. Some of that process I had
to learn by trial and error. At first I used fresh cow manure
to fertilize the soil. This resulted in the propagation of an
infinite number of weeds. I became a bit wiser and used
only chicken or turkey manure. I eventually got it right.

The last week I was there, I drove my electric cart
around the garden for one last view of the rich black soil.
Then, I looked out at the green meadows, the luscious
prairie grasses and wild flowers. I knew the land. I
couldn't walk anymore then, but at one time Jo and I had
touched and nurtured every foot of it. I sat there a long
time—somewhat in disbelief that we were leaving this
paradise. Finally I turned my cart around and without
looking back returned to the house.

Once the truck was loaded for California, we started
to work preparing all that was left in the house and
outlying buildings for the sale. The material had to be put
into lots that could be individually sold. The perfect
receptacle for display was a 2" x 12" X 18" cardboard box
used to ship pop cans or juice. They were readily available
at the grocery store, and were shallow, allowing easy
visualization of the contents. We tried to be creative in the
formation of the lots, placing one desirable item with
several less desirable ones—a newer coffee pot with an
older kettle, etcetera. Jo and I cleaned appliances, and
organized and prepared approximately 250 lots full of
household items. We were not convinced the auctioneers
would get through the immense amount of goods, but they
assured us the sale would move rapidly. I noticed when

the auction began, if a bid was not forthcoming on certain lots, two or three were pushed together and sold as one purchase.

A few days prior to the auction, after the sale bill circulated in the local papers, neighbors and town folks began to come by the farm for a preview of the merchandise. The sale bill, written by the auctioneers after they inventoried the house and grounds, was a 3 x 5 advertisement with about 1,000 words listing all items for sale. People must have read this with a microscope, as they came by to view items that had completely escaped my memory. I also realized that everyone does not buy retail. An older couple dropped by to look at the automobile for sale. They were driving a well-used Lincoln Town Car that they had purchased second-hand, but were thinking of "trading" as their car now had 186,000 miles on it. Our car had only 46,000 miles and was nine years old—a rung up the ladder for them. I understood the wisdom of their thinking.

The morning of the sale finally arrived. It was clear and crisp, and we thanked our lucky stars for a good day. That morning, Jo's brothers and sister and my sister and her husband came by to carry the merchandise out of the house onto the yard. The auctioneer and his helpers were also helping and, in about three hours, all the items were in place on the farm yard. We rented a 20' x 30' tent and six display tables to give the scene a little panache. Dan and the auctioneer worked out the traffic pattern so the influx of automobiles and pickups could be handled efficiently.

As a treat for all those helping, Jo drove to the neighboring town of Flandreau and to the popular bakery where she picked up some favorite baked goods. Thursday is the day the bakery makes popcorn balls, and I used to buy them routinely. In fact, if I didn't come in to get them, Mildred, my old friend, would call and wonder why I hadn't come. She knew my likes and dislikes and always saved a few fresh ones. Jo's favorite was the gold bar, a white cake with peanut frosting in the shape of a gold ingot. Her grandmother used to make them and through the years with all the company, Jo bought hundreds of gold bars. We had a habit of driving in with the pickup to the bakery, buying the cakes and popcorn balls and eating half of what we purchased on the drive back to the farm. It felt appropriate to devour them again on the day of the auction.

The sale was scheduled to begin at 3:00 p.m. on Thursday, September 24th. The mid-afternoon was chosen to allow working people to come. About 1:00 p.m. the auction RV (office) arrived at the farm and set up their equipment. The staff issued numbers to everyone attending the sale, while recording names and addresses in the computer. The bidding was done by number with no names involved. The back of the RV had bathroom facilities for men and for women. Shortly after the auctioneer arrived, a lunch wagon pulled in to sell sandwiches and soft drinks to the crowd, which by this time numbered approximately 200.

The morning of the sale we had an offer on the house and land. It did not take too long to decide. We accepted, as the couple making the offer were friends, and we knew they appreciated the beauty of the house and grounds. We also knew the property would be nurtured and loved—an important factor in our decision to sell.

At 3:00 p.m. everything was in place. There was a central speaker box that augmented the caller as he went from lot to lot with a portable microphone. The first auctioneer started by outlining the terms of the sale. All items were to be sold "as is" and paid for in cash or valid check. The auctioneer explained that the sale was like a marriage: "You take the item for better or for worse, but it is yours to have and to hold."

The auction began out on the meadow behind the barn where we had laid out fencing, gates, general farm equipment, and garden tools. The two auctioneers were excellent callers and took turns calling. They commanded the immediate attention of the crowd with their compelling patter of call: "I've got 50, 50, 50, who'll make it 60... 75?" Occasionally, one would get stuck on a bid and then would break the log jam by calling, "100, 100, 100... Now you know this item would cost you $800 new, and this article has hardly been used!" Then, mysteriously, the spell would be broken and the bidding would start again, "125-25-25-150-50-50-75," etcetera.

As the sale progressed, I observed how rapidly things moved. There was a sale every 30 to 90 seconds. Whereas land auctions are very leisurely, allowing the auctioneer to talk to all the bidders, this sale was moving rapidly, but not as fast, I understand, as a tobacco auction where a sale is made every 5 to 6 seconds.

The auctioneer keeps a patter (chant) of speech going all the time. This formulaic speech is so imbedded in his mind that he can recite it without thinking, using his cognitive powers to search the crowd for the next bidder. It can be compared to the sportscaster, announcing a horse race with reports on who is on the rail, who's on the outside, and who is in front while using his cognitive senses to watch for the unusual. Auctioneering is an old profession, dating back to the 19th century in England. It is male-dominated, usually passed from father to son. Such was the case with our auctioneer, who had developed the auction to an art form.

When there was a delay in getting the bid started, the auctioneer would cajole the audience with "Let's have a bid, you know it's only the last one that hurts." He would also bring up little sayings as in describing a tractor: "Folks, with the small number of hours on this vehicle, we can't even say it's been used, it has only been tested!"

The price received for some of the items caught our interest. An old dinner bell that we found in a barn when we moved on to the farm went for $200. But a hair dryer like that used in beauty parlors went for $1.50. The Tonka toys sold well but the art objects fared poorly. The auctioneers would not even put out a set of World Books. They said with the Internet, no one is looking at encyclopedias anymore.

The enthusiasm and energy of the auctioneers kept things moving along at high pitch for the entire five hours of the sale in progress. They went through the furniture, dishes, and toys, but the vitality really increased when they got to the tractors and car. This is why the heavy hitters, the buyers, had come. The lawn tractors and the larger tractor were all John Deere equipment in good shape. We had steam-cleaned them all, and checked each to make sure it would start and run on command. There was intensity on the bids. I watched one man march off angry and red-faced with disappointment saying, "Dammit, I thought I had it, too steep for me."

At this point, the two auctioneers, Chuck and Jack, showed their mettle as a team. While Chuck concentrated on one bidder, Jack would wheel around with great vigor and holler, "I've got $475." And so they would parlay the bids back and forth keeping up the energy while the bidders were so intense they were barely making a nod for a bid.

Finally the Cadillac, the last item on the sale, came up for bid. It was 7:45 p.m. and the evening shadows were falling. By spelling off each other throughout the day, the auctioneers kept up the momentum until this last item went on the block. The bids started and I noticed the couple in the Town Car had dropped out rather quickly. It finally got down to two bidders who were advancing cautiously and incrementally.

Again Jack and Chuck kept the energy high. When the bid hit $8,000. the one man must have reached his limit. Then came the final, "Going for 8,000, going for 8,000, going for 8,000... Sold!" As the sale ended and twilight approached, a hushed stillness came over the crowd. From a distance we heard a clatter and glanced up to see a flock of Canadian geese in V formation winging their way south for the winter. They were low enough that their wings made a soft whisper and their white striped necks were visible. In spring, they would return to their northern home. I felt as though someone kicked me in the stomach, and I uttered under my breath, "I'm sorry, I won't be here to welcome you back."

The remainder of the evening was spent watching the people load their wares into cars, pickups and trailers. Like ghosts in the night, they quietly, one by one, drove off the premises with their bounty on board. Their conversations were hushed, the air was still. Jo's cousins, Rosie and Bob, had purchased any number of odd articles and stayed until 10:00 o'clock loading their pickup. They lingered, reluctant to leave even if they still had a three-hour drive home. The night was dark as they pulled out with their truck strapped down, full of belongings that only a few minutes before had been ours. Rosie said, "I don't look back, and you mustn't either."

The hardest farewell was to Jo's brother, Bob, who took the kitchen table. He loved the farm and lived there during his cancer treatments in Sioux Falls. He used to say, "I don't need to go to heaven, I'm here." As he drove away, I could see his face and hear his sobbing. He died a few months later. As with Bob, there were many friends and relatives who gathered to support us that day—all with memories of good times at the farm. There were also a few who said they couldn't come as they could not bear to see us leave. Through family reunions, wedding receptions, medical meetings, summer holidays, retreats and traveling guests from many countries, we celebrated the beauty and bounty of living on the land and under the open sky.

After a few more goodbyes, we shut the door to the house and drove silently back to our hotel in Sioux Falls. When we reached our hotel room there was a bottle of champagne from our three children with a greeting that said, "Congratulations, we are proud of you." We had thought about them throughout the week—grieved and celebrated our memories. Only a few weeks before, they had all come for the 4th of July—traditionally a great event and that year especially memorable. We fixed fried chicken, calico beans, potato salad, melon balls and homemade ice cream with chocolate brownies—our traditional menu. The boys set off fireworks over the garden and we watched the sky as the small towns around us filled the night with color. Around 11:00 the sky was dark again and we could see the stars. We stayed up late identifying the constellations. No one mentioned that this was the last time we would be together at the farm. The children had agreed earlier that this was the best resolution for all concerned, albeit with heavy hearts.

The most amazing sight occurred the next morning when we drove out to assess the leftovers. We had been too tired to clean up the night before and the night was too dark. We had no idea what was left. Viewing the unlit grounds, which had been filled with merchandise the previous day, was surprising. It was as if a giant vacuum cleaner had come along and sucked everything away. Only a few of the card board boxes used to fill the various lots were in evidence. How amazing that people actually pay to haul away other people's stuff.

Three days later we were on a plane flying back to our home in Ross, near San Francisco. We had let go. Confident of our choices, we came back to the rose garden, the grandchildren, our books and our future dreams of a woodworking shop and a writing studio. Yet, the call of the auctioneer will forever ring in our hearts, reminding us that we must accept the reality of life without the farm. The chapter is closed:

Going

Going

Going

—Sold!

A Tribute To Brother Bob

Memorial Service, November, 1999

Robert Frost penned a verse that Robert Vaughn might have written:

> *The rain to the wind said,*
> *"You push and I'll pelt."*
> *They so smote the garden bed*
> *That the flowers actually knelt,*
> *And lay lodged—though not dead.*
> *I know how the flowers felt.*

While it may be true that you suffered most of your life, Brother Bob, you never lost your relentless optimism. You believed the buds of trees would open, you believed in grass in the days of snow, you understood why birds could sing. On your darkest days you believed in spring. You leave a legacy of hope for us all. Not the kind of hope that says everything will turn out the way we want—it certainly didn't for you, but the kind of hope that says God is with us and will never let us go.

I owe a lot to you, Brother Bob. Many times I felt as though I lived my life for you. You were always my advocate and believed I could do anything. No matter what I did or where I lived and traveled, you encouraged me. When I graduated from college, I thought of you. When I married Phil and had children, I thought of you. When I developed the feeding program for the poor and disadvantaged, I thought of you. And when I lived in big houses with trees, lawns and flower beds, I thought of you. You taught me to notice the sunrise, listen for the birds, celebrate a wild rose and welcome all people—especially the stranger. Thank you for walking through life with me. Memories of your benevolence forever linger.

Three weeks ago, when I told you good-bye, I wanted to say something profound. You were so sad. All that came out of my mouth was, "Don't cry, Bob." Later, I remembered a story from our childhood:

When I was a little girl, you never wanted me to be sad. You were my big brother and always protecting me. One day when I was crying, I remember you standing by the water bucket in the farm kitchen. You took the dipper, held it to my mouth, made me swallow and gently said, "Don't cry, Joanie."

I need that dipper today, Bob. I can barely swallow.

Happy Springtime.

I love you, Jo

Making All Things New

Faith is the bird that feels the light
and sings when the dawn is still dark

— Rabindranath Tagore

*This story of Lisa, the Hutterite girl who came to
live with us in 1972, is told in her voice. Since this
writing, the film <u>Hutterite</u> has been produced by Becca,
her daughter.*

Mary, the social worker, and my mother arranged
for me to run away from the Hutterite Colony. The plan
was for Mary to pick me up two miles down the snow-
covered road on February 6·, 1972. Two weeks earlier,
on January 15th my family celebrated my twenty-first
birthday, the age I was expected to be baptized and
make my life commitment to the German-speaking
Hutterite community. The date for the baptism was
arranged for later in February. I either had to run away
before then, or never. Mother knew I wanted a high

school diploma and to eventually become a nurse. I, Lisa, was the oldest of her ten children and although she depended heavily on me for help with the family, she also honored my desire to leave as there was no opportunity for me to stay at home and be educated beyond the eighth grade—a rule established by the Hutterite people. As a young woman I was expected to accept an arranged marriage, have a large family and live my life working within the community—the expectation of all Hutterite women.

My mother was miserable in the colony, often questioned and cried out, but always silenced or shunned. Although she recognized the warmth and security of the community, she was a smart woman, married to my father who had lost his way through alcohol, and she wanted more for her children. She thought if I could break away, maybe a new path would unfold for her family. In late December, she came upon an opportunity that would change my life and hers. My younger sister, Meg, broke her arm and the colony boss drove her, my mother and me to the office of Dr. Gross, a German-speaking orthopedic surgeon who practiced in Sioux Falls, a two-hour drive from the New Elm Springs Colony. Mother asked the doctor if he could do anything about the state law that only required students to finish the eighth grade. Dr. Gross, realizing that Mother confused him with his partner who was in the State Legislature, asked her specifically why this was important to her. Dr. Gross was aware of the colonies as his father, a county judge, had often done legal work and, on a few occasions, had taken him to visit the Hutterite communities. Mother explained that I wanted to go into nursing but could not get a high school diploma. She also explained that she had tried to arrange correspondence courses for me, but this was not met with approval by the colony officials and the process was stalled. She also mentioned the urgency of the problem because of the imminent baptism. She wondered if Dr. Gross could help us. After Meg's arm was put in a cast and we were about to leave, Dr. Gross walked us to the door and said, "I heard your question. Let me give this some thought and see if I come up with an answer."

A few days before Christmas, a card addressed to our family from Dr. and Mrs. Gross arrived in the mail. The Christmas card read:

> *Dear Mrs. Wipf and Lisa,*
>
> *My wife, Jo, and I would like to invite Lisa to come and live with our family until she finishes her GED and qualifies for nursing school. Let us know if this sounds reasonable and when we might expect her.*
>
> *Dr. and Mrs. Gross*

Mother waited until after Christmas and then called Mary, the social worker who had helped her with some of my father's problems. Mary called Dr.

and Mrs. Gross and told them she would drive me to their home if and when I decided to leave, probably February 6th. She then called Mother. Since the letter from Dr. and Mrs. Gross arrived, Mother and I had talked for hours, day after day, until my birthday on January 15th. Then, we made the decision that in order for me to leave, I must run away. There was no way the colony boss would grant me permission to go. Mother called Mary and the plan was made for me to walk away from the colony on Sunday afternoon, the 6th. Sunday was the better day as after church the young people had free time and often walked out on the road or down by the river on their own. I knew I could take nothing with me, only the clothes on my back. Because it was cold, I wore a light sweater over my Hutterite dress. My legs were bare and I did not have overshoes. Sobbing beyond control, I left Mother at the door and ran most of the two miles to the waiting car. We began the long drive away from the colony to my new home and in spite of how broken I felt, along with Mary's calm presence, I sensed an amazing grace and enough courage to believe I had made the right decision.

When Mary knocked on the kitchen door of the Gross home and we stepped inside. I must have looked pitiful as I recall Mrs. Gross gasped, then put her arms around me and welcomed me into the warm kitchen. By coincidence, several German speaking members from Dr. Gross' family were visiting that

afternoon as it was Grandma Gross' birthday. As I
entered the kitchen, I was surprised and comforted to
hear words of greeting spoken in German.
Throughout my body, I was chilled; my legs and
hands were red from cold and my face red from
crying. My stubborn curly hair was in total disarray.
Yet I will never forget the warmth of the moment and
the outpouring of hospitality and loving concern.
Even if I knew I had entered a strange new world, I
began to relax. We had tea and cake and the children,
Martha and Cort, showed me to my room on the third
floor of the beautiful English Tudor house. The baby,
Robert, looked on from his high chair. After the
relatives left, I gathered with the family in the living
room by the fire. Not long into our get-acquainted
conversation, we heard a heavy pounding at the
kitchen door. Mrs. Gross excused herself, went to
the door and then called, "Phil, come." By the tone
of her voice, I had a hunch who might be there.
Along with the children, I started for the kitchen.
Outside the door stood three heavy-set men in black
suits and the traditional black Hutterite hat. One
man, speaking in a gruff, deep voice, said, "Is Lisa
here?" Dr. Gross said, "Yes, she arrived a few hours
ago." Another man gruffly said, "Could we talk to
her?" Mrs. Gross said, "Yes, of course, please come
in." The three men sat at the round kitchen table and
Mrs. Gross beckoned for me to come into the room.
The children disappeared immediately and Dr. and

Mrs. Gross excused themselves.

Before me sat the colony minister, the colony boss and my uncle, the driver of the large truck parked in the driveway. In deep, gruff voices they all began at once to shout at me: "Why did you leave?" "Have you no respect for your people?" "Who do you think you are?" "You will amount to no good, end up on the street as a prostitute." No matter what I said, they yelled back at me. Soon I broke into tears. Mrs. Gross heard my sobbing and came into the kitchen. She said, "This is my kitchen and I will not have you speaking to this child in this way. Would you like some coffee?" By this time, Dr. Gross also came and sat at the table. The men began to insult him and ask rude questions like "Do you think you are a big shot doing this?" Finally, after slamming kitchen cupboard doors and banging a few pans, Mrs. Gross said, "Lisa will be just fine with us, we will take care of her and I think you should leave now." The men grumbled, stood up and reluctantly walked to the door. The minister turned to me as he left and said, "You will be hearing from us." And, I did. For several weeks they called and harassed me on the phone. Finally, Mrs. Gross told the men to stop calling, assured them I was fine and hung up. The harassment stopped. I later learned they had been very hard on Mother, which made me sad.

After they left, the family gathered around the kitchen table for hot cocoa. It was then we learned that Cort, age eight, had been standing behind the dining room door with his toy pistol listening to the men's voices. He was ready to shoot. We all needed a good laugh and relaxed as best we could. Then, Dr. Gross said an evening prayer and asked for God's blessing on the journey before us. The children gave me a big hug and I went to my room on the third floor. For twenty-one years I had slept in a room with six or more people. That night I was all alone. The room was very nice and I was comfortable, but, oh, so scared and lonely. I took a warm bath and lay in my bed staring at the dark ceiling. Who was I? Then, I began to toss, turn and sob again. Finally, I sat up, reached for the ream of paper and pen Mrs. Gross had placed on the desk and began to write. Who are the Hutterites and who am I for having grown up in a Hutterite colony? In bits and pieces, I wrote the following story of what I know about the history and culture of my people.

The Hutterites are a communal branch of Anabaptists who, like the Mennonites and Amish, trace their roots to the Radical Reformation of the 16th century. Based on the New Testament book of Acts, Chapter 2, tradition is based on a communal lifestyle. Strict pacifists, members are forbidden to participate in any kind of military activities, including military dress or contributing to war taxes. Theologically, the culture denies anything carnal and believes life on earth is to be endured as a brief interval before salvation and eternal life. All goods are held in common. The churches are plain and living spaces are small without adornment. Uniform clothing in which men wear black pants, no belt, a shirt, and suspenders, and women wear long patterned dresses with aprons and a polka dot kerchief have long been the traditional dress. After marriage, the men grow a beard and are the supreme authorities of the household. Women and children are taught to be submissive to this absolute patriarchal pattern.

Under the leadership of Jacob Hutter, the original community formed in the Tyrol of Austria. In 1536, Hutter was burned at the stake for his beliefs. Gradually, the community was forced to migrate to Transylvania and on to the Ukraine in Russia. Wherever they lived, their tenets of belief provoked neighbors and led to persecution. Finally, with the fear of Russia's newly initiated compulsory military service, the Hutterites inquired into the migration of people to the United States. The authorities assured them that they would be protected from war and military service. In 1874, the first colony migrated to Yankton, South Dakota. After almost 100 years in this country, my family continues to speak our own German dialect, the language of Jacob Hutter.

Before long, other colonies came to this country and up until WWI all flourished and enjoyed their religious freedom. An incident from the war changed the new world experience. I recall my grandfather telling the story never to be forgotten among the Hutterite people. During the early months of WWI, four colony boys were called into service and, because of their religious conviction, refused to wear the uniform. The young men were imprisoned, first at Alcatraz, and then transferred to Leavenworth Military Prison, where they were tortured. Two brothers, Joseph and Michael Hofer, eventually starved to death. Their bodies were placed in the uniform they had refused to wear and sent home to the colony. As a result of this deplorable incident, with the exception of the mother colony in Yankton, all the colonies moved to Canada. Over time, laws protecting conscientious objectors were passed and many of the colonies returned to the Dakotas and Montana. My community returned to its original homestead. Through the years, we often traveled to Canada as there was a close connection between all the colonies. The interaction between colonies, especially for the young people, provided the only social experience we had. Marriages were often arranged during those visits as well as other colony business exchanged. I was always glad to ride along with the elders and be a part of these social exchanges as they were some of my happiest times.

Since I know I will be asked many questions about my people, it is important for me to clarify how and what makes for colony life. Traditionally, the population of a colony numbers 100 to 150. When the numbers exceed that, the colony is divided in half, new property is purchased and half of the population moves and starts a new colony. This causes hardship as families and intimate friends are often divided. All the colonies are rural and self-sustainable. Food is grown and preserved, clothing is handmade and bedding and pillows are made on site, as well as brooms, aluminum pails, steel boxes for trucks and any number of farm tools, from the light industries developed requiring little overhead. Animals and poultry are important and the growth of pigs and cattle and especially turkey processing have become a marketable industry. There has been little change from tradition in the way the homes are built and lived in—yet the change in agriculture equipment has kept up with the current trends. Initially, women did their personal washing by hand as there was no running water, plumbing or electricity until the mid-1940s, and then only the communal kitchens and sewing centers had these conveniences.

Some conditions have improved but the daily labor for the women is intense, especially the gardening and preserving of food. The positive outcome from the structure was the interaction and sense of community. We all ate together, slept together and raised the children together. The whole colony was a family. Without question, we kids ran from one house to another. The schoolhouse was one of the colony buildings and all children were required to attend through eighth grade. After the eighth grade, the boys worked all day in the fields and among the animals, and the girls learned to work in the kitchen and sewing room. The teacher came from outside the colony, and the school was fully accredited according to the state educational requirements.

Politics and government were fierce. The minister was the head of the hierarchy. His secretary wrote the checks and took care of the business. The assistant minister helped with preaching, but served mainly as the "German teacher" for school-age children. I remember him as being very gruff and harsh. Along with teaching German he was the designated disciplinarian for the children. His role was set apart from the regular school program and he used his independence to impose severe rules of conduct. We were all afraid of him as he would use a belt to lash us if we misbehaved in the slightest way. Actually, the colony had many "bosses" such as a farm boss, the hog boss, the turkey boss, etcetera, depending on the various areas of specialization within the colony structure. Most of the business transactions required a vote by the community; that meant only the married men were allowed to cast a vote.

The domination of the men in the society is what bothers me the most about the Hutterite culture. Women are expected to bear as many children as possible and do the hard work of feeding and clothing the family and under nearly primitive conditions. The older women taught the younger ones. After eighth grade, I entered an informal apprenticeship and worked alongside the older women. I learned gardening, hoeing, and preserving, and I helped harvest acres of fruits and vegetables. As women, our task was to provide the food for the 150 colony members. Sewing, needlecrafts, knitting, cooking and baking were all taught on an informal basis. For eight years, I worked with a team of younger women learning from the older women. For the most part, we were separated from the men. The men tended livestock and plowed, planted and harvested the fields. They had use of air-conditioned tractors and combines, while the women hoed the fields by hand, and were covered from head to toe in long, hot, flowing costumes. What we put on our bodies was dictated by the men and colony tradition. While adhering to the clothing rules was tedious, I was bothered more by the attitude of the men toward women. We simply had very little freedom and were coached to speak softly. I expect, over time, conditions will improve, but the fundamental tenant of colony life defines the role of women as subordinate and submissive to male dominance.

Yet there are many aspects of the culture that I honor. As I lay in bed that first night away, so many images came to mind, especially the interaction with the older women. We worked hard but we also took care of one another as one large family. I will not forget the process of making goose down pillows, how we gathered the feathers, washed and dried them and stuffed the pillow sacks. There were feathers flying in all directions and the memory of running through them as a child lingers. Although the hours of preparing and preserving food were tedious, the satisfaction of seeing hundreds of jars filled with pickles and vegetables made us proud. And I loved the aromas coming from the kitchen—especially the homemade breads. We always had roasted duck on Sunday which meant that much of Saturday was spent butchering and preparing the ducks for cooking. Perseverance and endurance were taught by example and I am indebted to the older women. Their commitment to duty and responsibility will forever live in my heart.

Traditions are the key to efficient communal living; by doing the same thing day in and day out, tight structures are formed and no questions asked. Even the minister preaches the same sermons year after year. The sermons are taken from a small library of books dating back 450 years. And unbelievable as this all sounds, there is a feeling of security in routines. I expect this is the strength gained from the discipline of duty and I know this strength will follow me as I journey through the years ahead.

Morning came and as I laid aside my writings, I sensed a feeling of peace. As a result of my writing and my long dark night with my soul, I gained strength and confidence. I would walk down the two flights of stairs, meet the family and begin a new day. I had so much to learn, there was little time now for self-pity. As I turned to leave the bedroom, I glanced in the large mirror over my dresser and thought, "Maybe someone will help me do something with this head of hair." Then I took a small piece of paper and in bold letters wrote the words PERSEVERE. I stuck the paper in the corner of the dresser mirror and left the room.

As time went along, and I began my studies, I grew lonelier on third floor. Dr. and Mrs. Gross thought they were doing me a favor to offer me a quiet space, but I was miserable. One night they heard me sobbing again and Mrs. Gross rushed up to ask me what was wrong. I explained that I was so accustomed to communal living with no closed doors and constant conversations going on around me that I thought I was going crazy being so set apart. She immediately invited me downstairs to study among the hubbub of the family. The problem was solved.

The learning curve for personal habits was steep and my hair was a mess of curls and totally out of control. I couldn't help but remember the time the German teacher lashed me with a belt because of my curly hair. He thought I should be able to straighten it out. Mrs. Gross gave me a hair brush and said we would go for a cut when I was ready. She also found sweaters and skirts and stockings for me. I learned about the need for deodorant in a rather humorous way. One evening as we were eating dinner, Cort said, "Lisa, you stink." He was just being honest, but, of course, I was disturbed. Upon noticing my red face, Mrs. Gross jumped into the conversation and said, "Lisa, I have some deodorant and other products that will help you." That night we had a long talk about personal hygiene. I knew my ways were strange and different, but I was learning. I had never had a bathroom before and the room soon took on an element of self-discovery.

By speaking only English with the family, my vocabulary increased and even though my accent was apparent, I quickly began to think in English and found my studies easier. Through a correspondence course from the American School out of Chicago, I was moving quickly toward completing my diploma. Dr. Gross arranged for me to work in his office so I could earn my own spending money and start to interact with other people. In a few months, I successfully completed the high school course work, wrote the exams and earned my GED. As I adjusted to life away from the colony, I made new friends and met new expectations. I struggled to study and learn as I began exploring the availability of nursing schools. Since I had never taken chemistry, I was told that I could not possibly be accepted into a registered nurse program. I applied and was accepted into a Licensed Practical Nurse program and placed on a lengthy waiting list. I would have to wait at least a year before I could begin my nursing career.

During the year with Dr. and Mrs. Gross and their

family, I began to emerge from the life I had known. As a way of showing her appreciation to the Gross family, my mother arranged to have a set of six goose down pillows made. The only hitch was that I had to come to the colony and pick them up. The story is worth telling as seven months had passed and this would be my first return home. Mother smoothed the way and told me she was certain I would be welcome and hoped that either Dr. or Mrs. Gross would drive me to the colony. Mrs. Gross agreed to do so. She decided we would be more comfortable driving the family pickup as the Hutterites do not drive cars. Unfortunately, we awakened to a rainy August summer day. The skies were dark and gloomy. I thought it was a bad omen, but Mrs. Gross convinced me that it was a good day as the women of the colony would be relaxed and likely inside the house. She was certain they would all be glad to see us. Her encouragement lifted my spirits—yet I was full of fear. As we drove into the colony, I slid down into the floorboard of the pickup. I began to sweat and cry. Mrs. Gross spoke softly but firmly and told me to get back up on the seat as she needed me to give directions. The road was unpaved and muddy. The wheels of the pickup began to slide as the engine roared through the soft, wet dirt. I said, "There it is, that's my house." As the pickup stopped, the door of the house opened and my siblings came running and screaming to greet me. Mother, my grandmother and several older women friends stood and moved toward me as I entered the familiar room. I felt relief and great joy. They served a delicious poppy seed bread and coffee. We did not stay long as the weather was foreboding, and I was anxious to leave before the men realized I was there. We put the pillows in plastic bags and tossed them into the back of the pickup, embraced those who came out to say goodbye and made a speedy exit past the other buildings and out to the main road.

It would be many more months before I returned to the colony. In the meantime, my family began coming to me. One day we even made mint jelly in Mrs. Gross's kitchen and often we would look out the window and see my brothers driving a large truck and turning into the driveway for a brief visit. I had left home for new beginnings but realized a way to stay connected with my family would forever be provided. I began to walk with a lighter step and in due time I moved into an apartment and began my studies to become a nurse. I knew I could count on Dr. and Mrs. Gross for encouragement and guidance, but they knew it was time for me to be on my own. Shortly after my 22nd birthday, I left their home through the door I had entered the year before.

EPILOGUE

Forty-six years have passed since I ran down that snow-packed country road and away from the colony. After I left the Grosses I graduated from the LPN training, and worked a few years until the program was phased out. Then I took a two-year job with a mobile thermography program for the State of South Dakota. It was an intense program and involved daily travel which led to a nomadic lifestyle. We not only gave mammograms to fifty women a day, but collected data, trained volunteers, and answered hundreds of questioners.

Although the program gave me amazing experience, after two years I was ready to be settled again in one place. I accepted a position with the Surgical Intensive Care Unit at McKennan Hospital. Later that year, I met and eventually married Jack Flinn, a wonderful man who understood and supported my dreams of furthering my education. With his encouragement, I enrolled in advanced nursing programs to receive both my RN and my Master's degree in nursing. Most of my work has been with the Sioux Falls Veterans' Hospital.

Jack and I also built our dream house and started our family. We have two beautiful daughters and at this writing, Analise, the older one, is a highly specialized nurse working in San Francisco. She is planning her wedding in Napa, California. The other daughter, Becca, works in Hollywood with the entertainment industry. Officiating at the Napa wedding will be Mrs. Gross, our friend who helped me start on my numinous journey. Dr. Gross will also be at the wedding and maybe Cort, who helped me grow up that year in the family household. Robert, the younger boy who was a baby at the time I lived with them, is also invited. We have seen the family through the years and they continue to be interested in what I am doing, especially my recent years of working with returning veterans of the Iraq and Afghanistan wars. I have been honored for my leadership role in this area. Dr. and Mrs. Gross say they are very proud of me and, to be honest, I am proud of myself. I am also grateful that I could help my parents and siblings. Not without pain and difficult transitions, but with courage, nearly all of my family of origin left the Hutterite Colony, including my sister, Meg, the "little girl who broke her arm." She will be coming to the wedding and is eager to see Dr. Gross again. My father died at age 57 and Mother went on to take a few nursing courses and after receiving her Licensed Practical Nurse credential, also worked at the Veterans Hospital. Several of my siblings live successful, happy lives far away in mind and body from the colony. Others grew discouraged and moved back. Life has not been easy for any of us, yet as children we learned to endure and that quality alone has given us great incentive.

I have never given up my sense of responsibility for my brothers and sisters, and being Hutterite is something we all carry with us. Our children are different but understand our allegiance. I could never return to living within the Hutterite community and I am very grateful for the opportunities I have been given. And I am also grateful for who I am and recognize that the person residing within my soul retains Hutterite characteristics and values, which I am proud to claim.

I am not who I once was, all things are new, yet in so many ways all things remain the same. May God forever bless my people and bring light into the dark places of their lives. I will always love them even if they are tradition-bound and locked into their own story. At least, after all these years, they have accepted mine.

Lives and Experiences I Carry With Me

Their story, yours and mine—
it's what we all carry with us…
and we owe it to each other to respect our stories
and learn from them.

— *William Carlos Williams*

Ashok Banskota

Saving Children, Changing Lives

The miracle is not to walk on water but on the earth

— *Thich Nhat Hanh*

The rugged terrain that gives the Himalayans their beauty can be a barrier to medical care for the people who live there. Ashok Banskota grew up in the Himalayans and as a four-year-old, along with his parents and two brothers, walked the long distance to Kathmandu, where the boys were tested and accepted into St. Xavier's Catholic School—the only private school in Nepal. All three boys eventually graduated from high school and went to college and medical school in New Delhi, India, and on to the United States for specialty training. All three planned to return to Nepal. Ashok was the only one who did. He had not forgotten his father's heartbreaking stories of Nepal's poorest children, especially the rural disabled who were left alone all day while their mother worked. He was made aware of how they suffered emotionally and how they were made to feel unwanted because of their disability. The nearest health clinics were days by foot and no doubt understaffed. Ashok remembered these stories and wanted to help save the children.

He completed his orthopedic surgical residency at the Albert Einstein Hospital in New York City and became Board Certified, which allowed him to practice anywhere. Ashok made the choice to return to Kathmandu where he started a makeshift orthopedic practice, alone, for poor and disadvantaged children. His deep compassion and total commitment to every child in his care captured the attention of an American thoracic surgeon, Dr. Archie Fletcher, director of the mission hospital where Ashok performed surgery. Dr. Fletcher was concerned that Ashok was working too hard and needed help and encouragement. He also had reason to believe that Ashok's family was urging him to return to the United States where life would be easier for his wife, Padna, and their three young children.

Through his contacts with the Presbyterian Volunteers in Mission program, Dr. Fletcher signaled the need for help. He asked the question, "Were there any orthopedic surgeons who might be interested in coming to Katmandu as a short-term volunteer to work with Ashok?" He went on to say, "Someone who might revive the soul of Ashok so we can keep him here—he is a beautiful young man and we need him."

Phil and I had talked about taking a sabbatical and working as volunteers in a medical mission. After twenty years of a successful but intense medical practice, Phil was tired. He had developed the total hip replacement, given dozen of papers for the Association of Bone and Joint Surgeons and was badly in need of a break. At that time, medical sabbaticals were rare in a Midwest private practice. Phil liked to tell the following story of why he needed the sabbatical.

> A man was riding a horse. He was riding the horse very well and going very fast. When asked where he was going, the man looked over his shoulder and said, "Ask the horse!"

Nepal had always been an option for a sabbatical. We had come across a compelling book, *The Fabulous Flemings of Kathmandu,* a true story of a physician who, in 1956, had helped create Shanta Bhawan, the first modern hospital in Nepal. We were intrigued with the possibility of working there and living in Kathmandu, but we needed an invitation and we needed contacts and more details.

After applying to the Volunteers in Mission program and listing Nepal as a possibility, we were amazed and delighted when an invitation from Dr. Fletcher came asking Phil to work with Ashok at Shanta Bhawan. We were also grateful for the assistance of the mission program as those involved made the necessary contacts for our arrival. Our church in Sioux Falls funded and shipped a large trunk of orthopedic supplies to Shanta Bhawan. The supplies were gifts of companies from whom Phil had previously purchased orthopedic equipment.

All the interested people and loving support was enough to make Phil jump off the horse, and we left for Nepal June 20, 1981. Robert was in fourth grade and went with us. Cort traveled to Nepal, and then left for his freshman year at Stanford. Martha was working in Palo Alto. Our home in Sioux Falls was well cared for by neighbors, and friends gave us a rousing farewell send-off.

Ashok was thirty-two and Phil fifty-two when they met on the dusty road in front of Shanta Bhawani hospital. There was an immediate pairing. Day after day they performed surgical procedures—mostly on disabled children. And day after day their relationship grew into a deep friendship. Some days they would take a break for lunch and walk to our house, a short distance from the hospital. I loved seeing them together and usually managed to fix them something to eat—not always easy with the scarcity of healthy food.

One of the recurring bone disabilities among grown children in developing countries is club feet. In developed countries, club feet are treated before a baby leaves the hospital—usually by surgery or a cast or both. In developing countries, it is common to see grown children with club feet that have never been reconstructed. Phil was aware of a new procedure developed at the University of Iowa medical school that was designed to correct club feet in adults. Ashok was unaware of the method. Because of the far-reaching effects, Phil's teaching of this procedure was probably his signature surgical contribution to Ashok—who took to it like a duck to water. Even in the short time we were there, Ashok developed a reputation for correcting club feet. After we left, and throughout the ensuing years, patients came to Katmandu from many distances for this procedure. Ashok's orthopedic practice of reconstructing deformities affecting the lives of children became well known throughout South Asia. Of utmost importance is the awareness he continues to bring to the world regarding the plight of poor children in developing countries— especially the children of Nepal.

As Ashok's reputation grew so did support for his work. He was given the Humanitarian Award from the World Health Organization as well as distinguished recognition and support from the American Himalayan Foundation located in San Francisco. He travels extensively to speak of his work.

Approximately twelve years after we left Nepal, Ashok's dream of "The Hospital and Rehabilitation Center for Disabled Children" was created. The Center is located a few miles out of Kathmandu and is a world-class orthopedic hospital where 20,000 of Nepal's most disadvantaged children are treated yearly. To quote Ashok's son, Dr.Bibek Banskota, an orthopedic surgeon who joined his father a few years ago and is carrying on Ashok's dream, "It is staggering that 27% of the children in my country under fifteen years of age have some form of disability."

What is unique about Ashok and his son, Bibek, is their compassionate approach to care for the whole child.

They do this by combining spirituality with surgery, physical therapy, and in-house crafted prosthetics. They strive to care for the body, mind and spirit of the patient and embody their informal motto, "love heals."

Our family is enriched by the visits from Ashok and his family and in recent years by Bibek alone. They are often featured at events through the Himalayan Foundation and we are privileged to be invited. The first time Ashok returned to the United States and San Francisco as a luminary, he was asked, "Is there anything you would like to do while you are here?" Ashok replied, "Only one thing. I would like a driver to take me to see Dr. and Mrs. Gross." Alas, this was a touching moment to notice in that Ashok, although celebrated, was still the same kind and thoughtful man we had always known.

When I think of Dr. Fletcher requesting help to "revive the soul of Ashok," I smile. I know Phil's skill, ideas and encouragement inspired Ashok but I am not certain whose soul was revived—Ashok's or Phil's? I expect both. I know Phil helped to launch Ashok into an extraordinary future and Ashok gave Phil a blessing that stayed with him throughout his remaining years.

Bibek, who was five years old when we met him, is following well in his father's footsteps. After the 2015 earthquake in which he and Ashok organized the medical community to treat survivors, Bibek was also given recognition from the Himalayan Foundation and the World Health Organization. What a deep joy we felt to see this fine young man receive these awards and how we value his visits. Yet when we are with him I cannot help but remember a five-year-old boy with his parents and brother and sister on the dusty streets of Kathmandu.

In 2012, Robert represented us by attending the dedication of a wing in the hospital named for Phil and me. Mounted on a wall is a plaque with a photo of Ashok and Phil. The inscription reads:
Dedicated to this everlasting friendship…
And so it will be.

ADDENDUM

I would be remiss to write about Nepal and not include some of the details of how we lived, what we did and how being there impacted our future:

When we arrived in Nepal, we were greeted by Dr. and Mrs. Fletcher. They were incredible in their care for us. We were placed in a mission dormitory for a week until a house became available for our five-month stay. The occupants were missionaries who were going on leave. Fortunately, the home came with a cook, but there was seldom electricity and very little water. There was no refrigerator and only a small hot plate for cooking. A daily trip to the market was necessary. Fortunately, the cook had been trained by western standards and was aware of hygiene and cleanliness. However, he did surprise us from time to time when he rolled out the chapatti on the hard-packed dirt floor or sorted the rice on the floor to pick out the rocks. Our diet consisted mostly of rice called dahlbot, with a gravy, vegetables and, when available, water buffalo. Nepal, a Hindu monarchy, is mostly vegetarian. There were no dairy products. We were fortunate and did not get sick as many westerners do. We credit Depok, our cook, and we followed our simple rule: "If... you can't boil it or peel it, don't eat it." The diet meant no green leafy vegetables. The water was also in question as it contained Giardia, a small microorganism that the Nepalese tolerate well—but not westerners. We boiled our water and ran it through a ceramic filter. When visitors came, our treat to them was a glass of cool, clean water. We ate out only on rare occasions and had a rating for the restaurants: If you had been there three times without getting sick, it was a three star restaurant. If in two visits you were sick, it was a two star. And, if you were sick the first time, you did not return.

All day and through the night there was a parade of people who walked by our house, which was on the main road to the downtown area. A Hindu shrine stood close to our front door and women came with marigolds to place on the base of the shrine—which usually featured one of the many Gods worshiped in the Hindu religion. Along with people and animals moving through the night, we became used to hearing dogs howling and seeing monkeys everywhere. One morning I looked out and noticed a young boy on an elephant. I recall the elephant swaying along and the young boy singing—as if they were in rhythm.

Robert went to the Embassy school and thoroughly

enjoyed the cultural exchange with a variety of children belonging to diplomats and government workers from all over the world.

The first time the clouds opened revealing the Himalayas, I was overwhelmed by their immensity. It was mid-October and the sky surrounding Kathmandu was totally filled with huge mountains. We took three treks while there and better understood the unforgiving geography that keeps the rural people from access to proper medical treatment. We understand that now, through Ashok's vision and hard work, extensive outreach programs are in place and the premier pediatric orthopedic hospital he founded has healed over 75,000 children.

It is difficult to grasp the mountains and the rural areas without trekking through them. We were fortunate to have an amazing team of Sherpas and yaks that made our treks relatively easy and memorable. I am still humbled to remember the faces of the children and the hard-working mothers we met along the way.

There is an overused—but accurate—expression regarding Nepal. It goes something like this:

> You will never change Nepal,
> but Nepal will change you.

This was certainly how we regarded the outcome of our tenure there—memories of masses of people, the Himalayas and the unique purpose of our being there, forever lingers. We were given amazing grace with good health and enough energy to feel useful and make a difference in the life of Ashok Banskota and his family. Yet, we received far more than we gave. Perhaps our greater impact came when we returned home. We told the story again and again and our listeners always wanted more. Through our many photo slides and intimate stories of the people, we taught awareness and encouragement to those who wanted to do something similar. A few years after our return, I was asked to be the founding director of a feeding program for the poor and disadvantaged in and around Sioux Falls. The model developed—known as The Banquet—touches thousands of volunteers and continues to feed thousands of people. Similar programs are promoted in rural areas across South Dakota—land of my childhood. The commitment to develop this program was greatly inspired by Ashok's story and the faces of hungry children in Nepal—faces resembling the Native American children who frequented The Banquet. Phil became more interested in public health and global medicine. Our three children were also impacted by the Nepal experience and have chosen work which contributes to the common good.

I am grateful.

Crackers, Peanut Butter and Thin Gray Soup

I've learned that people will forget what you said,
people will forget what you did,
but people will never forget
how you made them feel.

— *Maya Angelou*

During our early days of living and working in Kathmandu, we experienced severe culture shock. Even though we traveled a month in India prior to our assignment at the Shanta Bhawan Mission Hospital, we were not prepared for what we encountered on the streets of Nepal's largest city—we were dazed, often terrified and clearly disoriented.

One noon hour as we walked toward our meager residence past Hindu shrines, monkeys, goats, rickshaws, and hundreds of people, we heard a voice call out, "Would you like to come in for lunch?" Amelia, a neighbor and longtime missionary whose husband was also affiliated with the hospital, recognized us and offered hospitality.

As we climbed the rickety wooden stairs leading to their sparsely assembled home, Amelia waited at the top and embraced us and motioned for us to sit down at a small, bare wooden table. After a few steps backward to a makeshift kitchen, she returned with three white bowls of thin gray lukewarm soup. She stepped back again to bring a jar of peanut butter and a few white soda crackers. For over two hours, we sat at her table absorbing the emotional safety and her thoughtful insights attached to living in a developing country. Her tender act of kindness had tremendous power. With lifted spirits, we descended the rickety stairs to the vibrant moving street crowd. We felt braver and stronger for having been there.

Since that long-ago day in Kathmandu, I have consumed many bowls of gourmet soup with generous accompaniments. Yet the memory of Amelia calling to us, our climbing the stairs, a few white crackers with peanut butter and a bowl of thin gray soup lingers.

Ajit and the American Dream

Hope is the door from one reality to another.

— Jim Wallis

Ajit Bhave was nine years old when we met at his parent's home in East India, a day's drive from Kolkata. A slight, handsome boy with vivid deep black hair and eyes, he came running barefoot to greet us. Our family was in route to Nepal where we planned to work at a mission hospital and stopped in India to visit Ajit's family. We knew Ajit's father who, in 1965, lived with us for a year. He was thirty-five years old with a wife and small daughter remaining in India. Under the sponsorship of "The Experiment in International Living," Mr. Bhave came to the United States to complete a graduate degree in education at the University of South Dakota. In our country, at that particular time, the program designed to help foreign students with continuing education was popular.

After the completion of his studies, Mr. Bhave returned to India where he became the principal of a boys school in the remote State of Bihar. Ajit was born there in 1972. The State of Bihar is one of the poorest regions of India and during our two-week visit with the Bhave family, we learned and gained immeasurable insight into the primitive Indian culture, which was a tremendous help in preparation for the Nepal experience. Our younger son, Robert, was ten years old and he and Ajit ran and played easily together. Cort, our eighteen-year-old son, and Phil stayed close to Mr. Bhave and were awed at his ability to direct the school of six hundred boys crowded into a small rudimentary space. I engaged with Mrs. Bhave, observing her marvelous ability to work in a primitive kitchen and produce delicious food. She spoke very little but her body language told me all I needed to know: she was a hard-working, dedicated family woman who made her husband's work possible while she cared for the children and tended the home in an extremely challenging environment. (For fun, I counted her assortment of spices and curry which she kept in a medium-sized cupboard—there were fifty-six jars in all.) Through her efforts I learned to adapt to and appreciate the Indian cuisine and gained insight into the women living in a third world culture.

The weather was unbearably hot but by sleeping in mosquito netting, we managed to avoid the insects. Thankful and exhausted from the two rigorous weeks of orientation, including side trips of interests—markets, temples, sari shops, religious rituals and crowds of local people—we concluded our visit and flew to New Delhi and on to Kathmandu, albeit on the threshold of immense culture shock.

After five extraordinary months in Nepal, we returned to living and working in South Dakota. Our scant communication with Mr. Bhave continued but with few details of the family. The years slipped by. In the meantime Phil retired and we moved to Northern California. One Sunday afternoon in 1993, we had a surprising phone call: "Hello, this is Ajit, do you remember me?" In his early twenties and fresh from studies at an Institute of Technology in India, Ajit was in San Jose working for a high-tech Indian company. We quickly established a meeting date and he, along with several friends from India, drove to our home in Ross. Ajit looked the same as the little boy we knew twelve years before only taller, more mature, and very handsome. After that first visit, he came often and joined our family celebrations.

Mr. and Mrs. Bhave traveled to California to see Ajit before he married Manisha, a lovely young Indian woman. An unarranged marriage, against tradition, clearly Ajit and Manisha have a love relationship. For this reason, the marriage was questioned by the family, but not for long. Manisha is a beautiful young woman and it is easy to see that she and Ajit are a radiant combination of culture, history and modern India. They also adapted well to California. After a civil marriage in San Jose, the young couple returned to India for a traditional Indian wedding. Our family was fascinated seeing Manisha's wedding dress and the photos and hearing about the festivities.

Mr. and Mrs. Bhave came again when the babies were born. One year they were in our home during the season of Halloween and were absolutely mesmerized by the carved pumpkins and hundreds of costumed children and parents coming to our door for trick or treats. Halloween on Shady Lane in Ross is unimaginable with up to six hundred children running on the street.

Shortly after their second son was born in 2008, Ajit and family came to say goodbye as they had decided to move back to India. Ajit planned to work for the same company only closer to his parents. He wanted the boys to know their grandparents and be raised in the Indian culture. The grandparents would also care for the boys while Ajit and Manisha developed their careers. Following a spirited farewell party, we wished them well, albeit we were sorry to see them go.

After six years, in August, 2014, the summer Phil died, another phone call came saying the family had moved back to Palo Alto where the boys were enrolled in school. Ajit was still with the Indian company. They came to see me in the fall of that year and again the following year. More time passed with many changes and busy schedules. Finally, we met again the summer of 2017 when Mr. and Mrs. Bhave made one last trip to visit. Now in their mid to late eighties, Ajit flew back to India and accompanied them on their flight to California where they planned to stay four months.

Robert, Cort and I drove to Palo Alto to visit them.

Much to our joy and surprise, we found that Ajit and his family are experiencing the American Dream. They live in a stunning large house on a desirable street in Palo Alto. We were told the school district where the boys are being educated is one of the finest in the country. We also learned that Ajit now owns the Indian high-tech company and employs over one hundred technicians.

Among the many memories we shared that afternoon was the story of Mr. Bhave's first meal at our home in South Dakota. After traveling several days from New York, he and a fellow student arrived on a train—an hour later than scheduled. Phil had come home from the hospital to greet them, but was restless to leave when the hour stretched on. Finally, weary and worn, our guests arrived. Mr. Bhave had written ahead that he was vegetarian, but would eat a hamburger as his first American experience. We sat down to the table, said a brief prayer, and unfolded our napkins. Before I looked twice at Phil, he had eaten his hamburger and was standing to excuse himself. Mr. Bhave had yet to start eating. When I asked him what he remembered about the meal, he said, "I thought if I have to eat as fast as Dr. Gross I would never make it through the year."

The beautiful thing is that, without pretense, Ajit and his family remain the warm, restrained, interesting people they have always been. Mr. and Mrs. Bhave believe in education and through sacrifice and hard work they instilled strong values in their children. I am humbled to think of Mr. Bhave's time with us and how difficult it was for him to leave his young wife and family and come to South Dakota where the culture and weather could not have been more opposite. I marvel at his equanimity and modest reserve. At the time, I was so involved with my own family that I didn't realize how lonely he might have been. And, I am chastened to recall our visit in his primitive home, teaching and living a meaningful life while raising his family.

Following a lovely dinner, prepared by a personal chef, Mrs. Bhave and I stood together, apart from the others, in Ajit's lovely parlor. Attired in an exquisite green and gold sari, with vivid black eyes and her graying hair pulled back in a bun, as it had always been, we quietly visited. Shy, slight and short in stature, with some urgency Mrs. Bhave reached for my hands and measured her soft-spoken words. She wanted me to know that she was also educated with a degree in library science but had not worked outside the home. She glanced over at the elegant master bedroom where she and Mr. Bhave were staying and said, "I am very proud of Ajit, and I cannot believe I am here."

I couldn't resist putting my arms around her. All I could think of was how young and brave she was to stay behind that year so long ago, not knowing where her husband was going. I also thought of how she managed her primitive home in India and worked so hard to welcome us. All these years later she was standing before me trying to absorb her son's accomplishments. She exuded a sense of amazement and wonder, yet seemed bewildered as if what she was experiencing was far beyond her grasp. I felt a warm, deep compassion for her. I breathed a blessing of gratitude for our friendship, paused, closed my eyes and imagined a nine-year-old barefoot boy in a remote Indian village—running to meet me.

Tragedy — Travel — Triumph

You may call God love,
you may call God goodness,
But the best name for God is compassion.

— Meister Eckhart, theologian

The 2016 Zika Virus epidemic alerted my memory of a personal glimpse into the thalidomide tragedy which occurred in Europe during the late nineteen fifties and early sixties. The following accounts define insights and outcomes gained while living and working in Heidelberg, Germany, during a portion of this tragedy.

What is thalidomide? Often called "the greatest of all drug disasters," thalidomide was first marketed in 1957 as an over-the-counter drug in West Germany. The trade-name was **contergan.** The drug, developed by a German company and primarily prescribed and marketed as a safe remedy for anxiety, insomnia, gastritis and tension, was well received in post-war Germany where sleeplessness was prevalent and the society was known to be hooked on tranquilizers and sleeping pills. Over time, it was used against nausea and to alleviate morning sickness in pregnant women. Shortly after thalidomide was sold in West Germany, between 5000 and 7000 infants were born with malformation of their limbs. Other effects included deformed eyes and hearts, blindness and deafness. By 1960, due to impressive marketing and safety claims, the drug had reached 46 countries and caused major birth defects in an estimated 20,000 children. Of the reported cases only 40% to 50% survived. The main characteristic feature of those who survived was the absence of limbs— arms that looked like fingers and only stumps for legs.

In 1962, Phil was granted a Fulbright Scholarship and invited to work/study at the Orthopedic Children's Clinic, associated with the University of Heidelberg in West Germany. At the time, he had completed his residency in orthopedic surgery and was discerning whether to proceed with academic medicine or private practice or both. The invitation to join the medical staff at the Heidelberg hospitals for a year was compelling as there were over 2000 children affected by the thalidomide tragedy in the immediate vicinity of Heidelberg. The hospitals were filled and Phil was a part of a team of orthopedists recruited to help. He was the only American. Fortunately, he modestly spoke and understood the German language.

Neither Phil nor I had ever traveled to Europe, which made the ten-day Atlantic sea voyage a high adventure and worthy of mention—mostly because the ship carried only Fulbright scholars who were fascinated with the history of the ocean liner. Built in 1924 for a Swedish-American line, the *MS Gripsholm* was the first ship built for transatlantic express service as a diesel-powered motor vessel, rather than as a conventional steamship. During World War II, the ship was used actively by the International Red Cross as an exchange and repatriation ship, carrying Japanese and German nationals to exchange points where the ship then picked up US and Canadian citizens to bring home to the United States and Canada. With a Swedish captain and crew, the ship made 12 round trips, carrying a total of 27,712 repatriates. Exchanges took place at neutral ports: Mozambique or India with the Japanese, and Stockholm or Lisbon with the Germans. After the war, the *Gripsholm* was used to deport inmates of US prisons to Italy and Greece. In 1954, the Swedish line sold the ship to a German line, who renamed her *MS Berlin.*

Not only were the passengers fascinated with the history of the ship but the United States was also embroiled in the Cuban Missile Crisis. The Atlantic was not a good place to be right then. A combination of tension and jokes circled throughout the ship. Here is one: "This battered and beaten ship is so old that a rifle shot could easily sink us." Fortunately, the Cuban crisis was solved and we arrived safely in Bremen, albeit not without extensive sea sickness as the ship bobbed over the waves instead of pushing through them.

We quickly settled into a modest apartment on beautiful Panorama Strassa overlooking Heidelberg, and Phil began his work with children affected by thalidomide.

I accompanied our four-year-old daughter, Martha Jane, to kindergarten and stayed there with her for several months where we both learned a "kindergarten German." We also met interesting people and made friends who taught us important details regarding life in Germany after the war and how we might adapt. Only German was spoken and body language saved me from despair. The days were long as Phil left before 7:00 a.m. and returned after 7:00 p.m. However, this gave me the opportunity to study the language and culture, meet our neighbors, go to the markets and accommodate to our small kitchen with only a hot plate and an open window for a refrigerator.

Christmas Eve was the highlight of the year. Late afternoon, we walked with our neighbors to the nearby cemetery where candles were burning on every grave. There was a light snow and the stillness and calm of the night lives forever with me. Later, Phil asked me to go with him on evening rounds at the Catholic Children's Hospital. Our neighbors invited Martha Jane to stay with them. We drove through the light snowfall on the road that parallels the Neckar River with the gleaming historic Heidelberg Castle spread out above us. The air was fresh but not cold and I recall that we said very little. It was truly a silent night. When we arrived at the quiet hospital glowing with candles, we heard a choir of men's voices singing carols. With a sense of joy and gratitude, the nuns warmly greeted us. After stopping and listening to the choir, and trying to absorb the awe and wonder of it all, we walked to the wards filled with children. There, I saw for myself the ravages of thalidomide. The beds in the wards were lined within inches of each other and filled with small children with no arms or legs. There was little beyond obvious care that could be done for them. They would stay in the hospital until taken home, adopted or institutionalized. What I noticed was an essence of peace in the midst of tragedy.   There were a few family members, softly weeping, coming and going. As they, each one, stopped to thank us for coming on Christmas Eve, I could only imagine their heartbreak. Through their tears, I felt goodness and mercy as if they were wrapped in the Holy Spirit.

As this particular tragedy was addressed, Phil told me there was much to be learned from working with the medical team involved. Among the many creative ways of caring for these youngsters were the amazing designs for artificial limbs and body braces that were then created. These designs were quickly incorporated by orthopedic surgeons throughout the world and are now being used again for the Zika victims.

The following summer, we returned to the United States and Sioux Falls, South Dakota where Phil began his private orthopedic practice. Within a few short weeks he was shocked to attend a young boy in the emergency room who had lost both arms in a farm accident. Because of his access to the Heidelberg team of doctors, Phil was able to help the family find the needed resources to build the boy, Jimmy, two artificial arms. Through the years the family kept in touch with Christmas cards in which Jimmy drew pictures with the use of his artificial arms. After Phil retired and we moved to California, we lost contact with the family but knew they still lived in Iowa and that Jimmy went to college and then returned to the farm.

Approximately forty years had passed since Jimmy was carried into the emergency room when a cousin of mine, living on a farm in South Dakota, sent us a video of a national "Farmer of the Year" award being given to a young farmer in Iowa. The title of the video read: "A young man who lived and worked the farm with no arms." Along with the use of artificial arms, the video showed the 45-year-old farmer using his teeth to lift up certain items—even hay to feed his cattle. His name was Jimmy. I recall Phil weeping as he watched the video.

Due to the concerns for the safety of the thalidomide drug, Dr. Frances Kelsey, a reviewer for the U.S. Food and Drug Administration, refused to authorize the drug for market in the United States. Her concerns and delay were later justified. Dr. Kelsey's career also intersected with the passage of laws strengthening FDA oversight of pharmaceuticals. She was the second woman to be given the President's Award for Distinguished Federal Civil Service.

The powerful memories of Heidelberg and that particular Christmas Eve live on. I often wonder: what happened to all the children? The families? The Catholic nuns? The medical team? This I know: From the tragedy, lessons were learned, hearts were broken then assuaged from extraordinary acts of compassion, young doctors were wiser for having participated in the historic moment, other patients were helped from the medical outcomes, healthy babies were born again, life moved on. Is it enough? Maybe not, yet there is always inspiration gained from the resilience of the human spirit and the kindness of those who care.

We were privileged to be there.

After the Fog

Gratitude is the Memory of the Heart.

— *French Proverb*

We had never driven in dense fog. Friends told us California was full of sunshine and the Central Coast where we were going was one of the most beautiful areas in the country. Phil was reporting for two years of military duty. This was 1957 and he had just completed six years of medical training and decided this was a good time to take a break before he began his surgical residency. After directing a summer girl's camp outside of Ann Arbor, Michigan, where we lived, I left my position as program director with the YWCA. After the long drive from Ann Arbor, we arrived in Santa Barbara late evening but decided to push on to Vandenberg Air Base and the small town of Lompoc, approximately 30 miles away. We planned the trip to arrive on my birthday, October 5th, which we intended to celebrate along with the beginning of our new experience.

Our first evening in California was anything but a

celebration—we were disappointed and miserable. After we left Santa Barbara, the roads began to wind toward the ocean and the fog invaded the coming darkness. In the pitch-black evening, we crept along, not even sure we were on the right road. We could not see anything except our headlights. After two hours, we came upon a sign that said, "Ten miles to Vandenberg Air Force Base." We kept on and finally I heard Phil say, "We made it."

I had been looking for a sign taking us to a small Mexican inn that we had read about. Since we had never met anyone from Mexico and the evening was brooding with dim lights leading to the doorway of the inn, we admitted to being frightened. We stepped out of the car, and I thought I would freeze on the spot. We were seven miles from the ocean, and the fog and wind penetrated my summer clothing. I kept thinking of all the people who told me about the California sunshine. I started to tear up, which always alarmed Phil. He said, "Don't be sad, we're here." Then I realized he was very close to tears himself. We were exhausted. It was so dark and quiet on the small town streets, I wondered if anyone lived there. I wanted to go home. I thought even South Dakota and Michigan in winter would be better than this.

After speaking with the friendly innkeepers who offered us food and a warm room, we began to feel better and agreed that a night's sleep would put us back on track. After all, we were young, both in our twenties, and this was an adventure. Phil wished me "Happy Birthday" and kissed me goodnight. I said, "Welcome to California, morning will come," and kissed him back.

And, oh, my, what a morning! We awakened to a room full of sunshine with gorgeous fresh air coming in the windows. As we opened the door to the outside, we could see the brilliant blue sky and feel the warm temperature. The kind innkeepers came to welcome us again and offered us breakfast. They also suggested that we drive just a few miles out of town to see acres and acres of flower fields. We had read about the Burpee Seed Company but had no idea of the extent of beauty surrounding the little town. The fields were akin to a patchwork quilt with every color glowing in the sunshine. I couldn't believe what I was seeing.

Since it was Sunday morning, we decided to drive back through the small town and find a church, which we did, and one to our liking. Within minutes, we felt at home. Friendly folks from all corners of the church seemed to welcome us. Maybe we looked lost, and maybe we were, but their hospitality persuaded us to rejoice and be thankful. We had arrived and it was good. The decision not to live on the military base had already been made as we were there for a short time and wanted to live in a genuine community.

After a few days in the inn, we located a small apartment in Lompoc and Phil reported for duty at the military hospital. He enjoyed his colleagues and the variety of patients. I believe it was the only time in his long career that I knew him to be relaxed with medicine. We later spoke of this: the ensuing years were fulfilling and illustrious but not without the cost of heavy responsibility, sacrifice and strained health. We were also inspired by the people from the small community, including my neighbor from Mexico who taught me the Mexican cuisine, and those who managed the flower fields and worked on the nearby cattle ranches, strawberry fields, orchards and truck gardens. After years of academia, we were delighted to be with people who lived and worked on the land. We felt at home.

Among the hard-working folks we met during those memorable years were Gordon and Edithmary Davis. They managed and lived on a ranch several miles from town and could not always be in church. But one morning we were singing in the choir and after the service, while folding up our music, we noticed them. The two of them walked to the front of the church and asked if they could speak with us. They were a striking couple. Gordon was tall, weathered and handsome in a western shirt with bolo tie, cowboy boots and carrying a Stetson hat. A slender pretty blonde, Edithmary wore a colorful print dress. Her skin was radiant with energy and good health. They were about fifty years old. As we shook hands, we felt the familiar calluses of hard manual work and later commented at how they reminded us of the ranchers we had known from childhood. We were not surprised to learn that they had grown up in Nebraska and perhaps someone told them we were from the Dakotas. They also may have heard that we were looking for a house to rent as, by this time, we were expecting our first baby. They invited us to the ranch, where we enjoyed their marvelous hospitality and, in the spring, we rented their small cottage in Lompoc. They had no children and reached out to us akin to family.

Gordon and Edithmary were high school sweethearts, married in 1928, and they had moved to California as the Great Depression had seriously affected the Great Plains. They settled in Ventura County and worked on ranches there until they moved to Lompoc in 1940 when they were hired to manage the 16,000 acre Jalama Rancho for the Fred Bixby Company. According to journals from the Lompoc Historical Society, the ranch land overlooking the ocean was beautiful but had been neglected. Gordon and Edithmary turned the land into a thriving cattle business, but not without an immense amount of hard work. Cowboys and workers were hired to run cattle, build fences, install phone lines and modernize the buildings. The first year, 1940-41, was one of the wettest in California history—65 inches in one area of the land, and 49 inches at the ranch headquarters. Bridges were washed out and barns as well as trucks and cars were lost. The ranch was not accessible much of that year. Eventually Mr. Bixby purchased a bulldozer and the ranch crew started building roads. Within a few years, buildings were restored or built, with bunkhouses, barns and cottages, a dining room for the ranch hands and more, which all resulted in a spectacular gleaming white- and green-trim assemblage of buildings on a hill overlooking Highway 1 and the Pacific Ocean.

We were told that none of this would have been accomplished without Gordon and Edithmary. They were relentless in their devotion to Mr. Bixby and their willingness to fulfil his dreams for the ranch. We were fascinated by their stories and the others told to us. In the early years, Edithmary did the cooking for the ranch hands. She also managed the walnut harvest and the olive, grape and pear orchards. All of her hired help was male. Even when we visited the ranch, I do not recall seeing another woman. Her pet deer and the peacocks signaling arrivals coming up the hill were always an attraction. She kept the deer only until they were adults, and then turned them loose to roam the ranges with the many herds of deer that populated the area.

Gordon was still managing the reconstruction when we met him, and Edithmary was still managing the kitchen. I recall the pet deer: Bambi, Judy and Dottie, and the peacocks with their beautiful spread of feathers. By then, the ranch was known as one of the larger cattle producers in the area. We were there for the round-up when the calves are separated from the cows. I understood some of this as I grew up on a cattle ranch, but not one like this. There were hundreds of cattle and an impressive number of cowboys on beautiful horses—real cowboys, working the herds.

Edithmary arranged long tables of hardy food at noon. The men started the cattle drives at daybreak and were up long before dawn. They were hungry. We enjoyed watching them savor the refried beans, barbequed beef and mounds of potatoes, vegetables and fresh apple and carrot cakes. After the meal, I noticed several men slip away and sit down for a nap with their backs against a tree and their cowboy hats dropped down over their faces. We had taken a young family with two boys with us to share the experience. Johnny, one of the little boys fascinated by seeing a real cowboy, went up to one of the men dozing, tapped him on the shoulder and said, "Cowboys is my favorite game." I noticed him and remember an annoyed grunt that came out of the man, until he noticed Johnny. He then took Johnny's small, soft hand, placed it in his rope-scarred own, tenderly looked at Johnny and said, "Mine, too. "

How we enjoyed getting in the Land Rover and riding with Gordon over the hills. We had never seen live oak trees nor had we ever seen such beautiful land. The ocean glistened in the distance and I was overwhelmed by the wide-open horizon. I dreamed of returning and living in those hills.

Gordon and Edithmary's little town cottage was perfect for us. Our baby girl was born and they became her California grandparents. The two years slipped away far too quickly. After his orthopedic residency, Phil had marvelous offers to return to Santa Barbara. One doctor called him twice a year and was astonished when Phil did not accept his offer. I was astonished as well, but I knew in my heart that Phil was making the right decision in returning to South Dakota. Yet, for over twenty years, when Edithmary would send us ten pounds of harvested walnuts and photos of the flower fields, I would shed a few tears—just to remember her disappointment, and mine, that we did not return to the Santa Barbara area. She was so confident that we would.

After Gordon and Edithmary retired, they wrote and told us that Mr. Bixby had died and all the land was sold to developers. The ranch was gone and the hills covered with houses. We were deeply saddened to hear this. All the dreams and hard work to nurture and save the land and keep it natural and beautiful had vanished—violated by those with cost-effective power.

Among the memories and souvenirs Edithmary gave me was a fascinating cookbook, "Cowbelle Cuisine," presented by the Santa Barbara County Cowbelles. The mission of the women was to advocate beef production and the nutritional importance they believed it played in maintaining health. The book is filled with drawings of cows, horses, brands, barbed wire, bunk houses and lariat ropes—I regard the small book as a gem. She also gave me recipes for tamale casseroles, Mexican chili, refried beans and her signature entry—"the prize cookie."

Gordon and Edithmary gave us a glimpse of what mattered to Californians during the era when agriculture and land use had a strong voice in local government. They were also active in the local community, especially in regard to preserving the history of the land. Through their eyes we learned to love California—even the fog.

John Wabasha and the Banquet Story

We are all tied together
In the single garment of destiny,
caught in an inescapable network of mutuality.

— *Martin Luther King, Jr.*

John Wabasha, a Lakota Sioux Indian, regularly ate at The Banquet. He was a slight fellow with large dominant ears, a small head and a few wisps of black hair. His toothless grin was radiant and wide and his speech, even though altered by a lisp, was clear. The other men who came with John obviously enjoyed his convivial, caring and kind company. They called him Mickey Mouse.

John was around forty-five when I met him at The Banquet, where I was directing a feeding program to serve the poor and disadvantaged people in Sioux Falls, South Dakota. Designed to be a glorified soup kitchen where the poor would not be served poorly, the program was given the name "The Banquet." Developed in 1985, and located in an area of town where the homeless and low-income people gathered, the feeding program operated out of a refurbished space, previously a popular bar. On opening night a small curious crowd of 45 people came to eat. Over the next nine months the numbers jumped to over 300.

In 1996, I wrote a book, *The Welcome Table,* defining the model we created, which included tablecloths, napkins and fresh flowers on the tables—along with nutritious food. Our mission was to create a respectable place of hospitality in which both body and spirit would be nourished and a sense of dignity restored.

The key to our success was to organize and coordinate volunteer teams from across the community— housewives, teachers, bankers, doctors, lawyers, business associates, school children, etc.—who would purchase, prepare and serve the meal, then sit and eat with those who came. "The guests"—the term used—included women and men and families with young children. Approximately one-third were Lakota Sioux Indians who had left the reservations for a better life in the city. John was one of them, although he was different in that he was showered and well shaven, and had a part-time job as a janitor in one of the local banks. If I mentioned his name to any of my friends who had businesses in the area of The Banquet, the response was always a spirited, "Oh, yes, we know John Wabasha, he has come a long way." I never inquired as to what was meant by "a long way" but I suspect John had an alcohol problem as so many men coming off the reservations do. I only knew that I enjoyed sitting with John when he came to eat and I confess that some of this was because he was entertaining, endearing and pathetic with a touch of charisma that warmed my heart. He loved to talk and with his lisp he reminded me of a jack-in-the-box or a clown who just jumps out of his box and chatters.

One night I was brave enough to ask, "John, tell me a little about yourself, why are you here?" Thoughtfully, with a twinkle in his eye, he gave me his big grin and said: "Vell, Jo, I yike company and tis bether den tittin at the bar."

Along with dozens of stories from my tenure of directing The Banquet, I had not thought of John Wabasha in nearly thirty years—until recently while riding the Neustep machine in a fitness room. Usually when I ride those machines I try a number of things to keep from being bored—poetry, scripture, prayers for my children, meditation—anything that will get me through 30-40 minutes of exercise. But that afternoon, I was just plain bored when who should pop into my mind but John Wabasha. As I remembered him, I started to laugh and said to myself, "Well, Jo, dis is better den tittin at the bar." I finished the workout and smiled all the way back to my apartment.

I have no idea if John Wabasha still lives, but The Banquet, after thirty plus years, is astonishing. There are now over 20,000 volunteers and over 1400 serving teams serving up to 850 people nine times a week, including four breakfast meals and a Saturday lunch. In 2006 a new building was renovated to house the growing numbers.

The staff is paid and a new state-of-the-art kitchen and dining hall are in place. The boards are active and The Banquet is a member of The Sioux Falls Community Foundation. As more and more displaced, marginal and disadvantaged people come to eat, the program keeps unfolding. Serving groups from small towns in the vicinity of Sioux Falls, including Iowa and Minnesota, also participate. In 2016 a second program in a different location was organized to help accommodate the growing number of refugees coming from all over the world. School supplies, clothing and personal items are also donated. Old friends write and tell me amazing accounts of community support and I have been invited back a few times to offer my praise for the good work being done or to dedicate some new wing or phase of the program. I am always welcomed like some hero, and, of course, *I am not a hero*. I, along with a marvelous team, was simply inspired to develop and coordinate an organization that needed to happen. The community rallied and a program was built with far-reaching effects for both those who come to eat and those who come to serve.

As I continued my musings, my mind traveled over the years to the faces of the families and children and the poor elderly who frequently come and build a healing community among themselves. I wondered how many of the Indian families went back to the reservation and what has happened to their children. I recalled how I marveled at the capacity of the downtrodden to be thankful and joyful and at the mutuality established between "them and us." I could not forget that after a few minutes around the table, we were all "us" and the sameness that connected us was far more powerful than the differences dividing us. I wondered how much had changed in the community, if the barriers of race and class and the immeasurable pain of the poor and disadvantaged people would ever be overcome. Then, I thought of the opportunity The Banquet offers for understanding and awareness. Through this vast effort, seeds of trust are planted in the soil of the whole community and a glimmer of hope is restored. I recalled many stories, wonderful stories of courage and hope, pain and sadness, goodness and mercy, many I had not thought of in years. Until, one rainy afternoon on a fitness machine, thousands of miles away, my heart and mind remembered John Wabasha and with gratitude, I smiled.

Repairing the Fracture

Kindness is the greatest wisdom

— Anonymous

On a cold winter night, a few days before Christmas, Charlene, a thirteen-year-old Lakota Sioux Indian girl, and her mother and five brothers came to The Banquet, a soup kitchen in Sioux Falls, South Dakota. The roads were snow-packed and the drive from the Pine Ridge Indian Reservation had taken all day. Seeking a better life the hungry and homeless family came to The Banquet for help. They were given food and through the efforts of our volunteer team serving that evening temporary shelter was located. As director of the program, I spoke to a pastor of a local church and his congregation offered to sponsor the family and help them adjust to life in the city. They found a two-room house and provided necessary furnishings. The boys went to a nearby neighborhood school and Charlene walked alone to a distant middle school. On Christmas Eve friends from The Banquet gave the family a Christmas tree; others provided presents and food.

Later in the winter, Charlene fell and broke her right elbow. The boys ran for help and one of the workers preparing the evening meal at The Banquet took Charlene and her mother to the emergency room. Charlene held her elbow to avoid movement of the arm but although it was evident from the X-Ray that the lesion was painful, she displayed little emotion and avoided eye contact with the physician—who mysteriously happened to be Phil, my husband. With a patient load waiting, Phil interpreted the apathetic response to his brief explanation as a lack of understanding, and due to the complexity of the lesion; he chose not to further explain other than to tell them that surgery was necessary. He hastily gave the mother instructions in caring for the elbow following surgery and scheduled a return appointment in six weeks.

When Phil gave Charlene pain medicine she remained withdrawn. By now, he was aware that the family was frightened and had never been in a hospital before. He trusted that his staff would give them the proper orientation and left the scene. Later that evening, he operated on the girl's elbow and repaired the fracture by pulling the fragments of bone together with fine pins which protruded through the skin. A cast was then applied. After the procedure was completed, Phil found Charlene's mother in the waiting room and tried to explain what had been accomplished. He was impatient with her indifference but proceeded to tell her that Charlene would be in the hospital three days and the cast would have to remain in place six weeks. He pressed her to come back in ten days as he wanted to check the cast.

Charlene was seen during rounds the next morning. She continued to avoid eye contact with Phil and was strained and trembling. In spite of the swelling she admitted no pain. She was released from the hospital and did not return for her scheduled appointments. After four weeks Phil was concerned and made a note on her chart but had no way of contacting her as she had no telephone or permanent address. Although he was uneasy regarding the circumstances, the case was dismissed.

Throughout this time Charlene and her family had continued to come to The Banquet. I asked about her arm and noticed the cast was torn but had no idea she was Phil's patient. The family seemed happy and had made friends through school and The Banquet community, albeit the mother had not found work.

Phil seldom joined me at The Banquet as he was usually making evening rounds or preparing patients for surgery the next day. We would meet at home around eight o'clock for a late dinner. But one evening after he had dismissed Charlene's case, he said he would like to come and spend the evening. I suggested he stand at the door with me and greet the people. When Charlene and her family came through the line, I could tell that Phil was visibly surprised. Charlene looked at him and for the first time smiled. Her mother said, "Aren't you Dr. Gross?" Phil took a tray and joined them for dinner. He looked at the cast and said, "What happened, you never came back?" Her mother said, "We have not driven our car in months as we have no money for gasoline." Phil noticed that the cast was torn and frayed. He said, "What happened to the cast." Charlene said, "My brothers are trying to take it off with pliers."

Beginning to comprehend the circumstances, Phil was moved to do something. He made arrangements for Charlene to come to his office and the cast was removed. Fortunately, the X-Ray showed a healed fracture. The pins were removed with the understanding that to avoid the transportation problems Phil would see her from time to time at The Banquet. He began to come regularly and would often sit with the family. Charlene talked with him and told him stories about reservation life. The whole family took part in the relationship. When I could, I would join them. By year's end, however, the mother was discouraged from unemployment, poor housing and culture shock and took her family back to the reservation.

Charlene's story and the manner in which Phil handled the situation at the hospital became a source of revelation to him. He took the case to national orthopedic meetings and began a quest to study the health care needs of the poor. He felt an urgency to become an advocate for more comprehensive health care and included the ethics of the case. At the time, he was on the National Board of Ethics for the American Orthopedic Association. He used Charlene's story to illustrate his own omission as to what is ethical and what is unethical in patient care—especially in caring for the poor and disadvantaged patients.

As for me, I regard Charlene and her brothers as part

of the whole cadre of Indian children who came to The Banquet. Their beautiful faces never leave me. I suffered with them and to think of their plight I continue to be discouraged and feel a relentless melancholy. There is little hope on the reservations for the young people. I hear of a few individual cases in which basketball scholarships are given for higher education and organizations formed to help them break away from the realities of their environment—but there are few success stories. I am grateful for all those far and near who reach out to offer assistance. And I am grateful for The Banquet in Sioux Falls, that continues to welcome the Indian people and surround the children with kindness. The hundreds of people who come to serve learn empathy and awareness. The poor are not served poorly, and goodness and mercy prevail. The Banquet has touched thousands of lives and continues to renew faith that someday justice will reign and the barriers of race and class will be overcome. I am grateful for the opportunity I had to know the Indian children and for the insight received from Charlene's circumstances. Mostly, I learned that without understanding, differences create fear, and when moved to understand, differences enrich life.

Transforming Loss

We cannot afford to forget any experience,
not even the most painful.

— Dag Hammarskjold

The call came at 1:00 a.m. on June 2, 1997. It was
Paula, their daughter. In between sobs she related the
tragic events of her parent's death which had occurred
only hours before: On a fishing trip to Ontario, they were
flying into a remote lake to spend the week fishing. As
they came in for the landing, the wheels on the pontoons,
previously lowered to permit movement on the land, had
not been retracted. As a result, when the pontoons hit
water, the wheels' resistance caused the plane to flip over
with the body of the plane under water and only the
pontoons visible on the surface. The pilot had
miraculously escaped through a window but our lifelong
friends, Boots and Judd, remained trapped inside and
drowned.

As Phil and I listened to the report, we were shocked
and shaken into disbelief. As we tried to absorb the impact

of the message, we sat and looked at each other. There were no tears, just a gaping silence as if to say, "Was this really true?" I made cocoa and we stayed awake until dawn. By then reality had set in and we were making plans to return to South Dakota. There was never the question, "Should we go?"

Judd and Phil had known each other for fifty years. They met at a state high school event and again during their pre-med courses at the University of South Dakota. They were like brothers. Before exams and difficult assignments, they studied together and upon acceptance into medical school they shared the same cadaver. Although competitive, it never seemed to matter that who came out on top. They graduated first and second in their class. Phil remembered Judd for his brilliant mind, insatiable curiosity and marvelous sense of humor.

After five years at the University of South Dakota, they transferred for their last two years of medical school—Judd went to Northwestern in Chicago and Phil went to Washington University in St. Louis. Later Judd completed an ophthalmology residency in New York City and Phil an orthopedic residency in Ann Arbor. They both did a two-year stint in the armed forces.

By this time, both of them were married. While in undergraduate school, Judd asked me (Phil's girlfriend) to introduce him to "that black-haired beauty" in my sorority. Phil and I later participated in their wedding.

After all the education and training was completed, Judd and Phil with their families returned to South Dakota.

Judd joined his father's practice in Mitchell and Phil began
his work in Sioux Falls—seventy-five miles distant. We
were happy to be in the same area again and
communicated often. We each had a daughter and two
sons. Often when Boots and Judd travelled during the
winter months, we kept their youngest boy, Todd. We
enjoyed watching our families grow and shared in their
weddings, holidays and other special events. Their joy
was our joy and their sorrow, our sorrow. Little did we
know that the greater sorrow was yet to come.

As we flew across the country on Wednesday of that
mournful week, we braced ourselves for the hours ahead.
When we drove from the airport into the driveway of the
family home, all three children (all in their thirties) came
out of the house to meet us. Deep was their hunger for
comfort and explanation. They also had a list of things to
do and were obviously glad we had come to help. At the
moment they were waiting for and dreading the return of
the bodies from Canada to Mitchell. The funeral was
scheduled for the following Friday. Paula and I worked
on the obituaries and planned the service on Thursday
while Phil and the boys greeted the stream of visitors who
passed through the house carrying food and flowers. The
community was in shock and few words were spoken. By
late afternoon, the bodies had arrived and were ready for
the family to view. The community was invited to come
in the evening. The children, Paula and Mark, came with
their spouses but Todd was alone. I felt the need to go
with him. The three of them were brave and showed great

courage but I will never forget what Todd softly said to me: "Jo, these are just their bodies; they are not here."

The following day the crowds came early for the 11:00 service. The church was overflowing and many people stood outside or in the aisles. The parking lot was jammed. Phil and I went in with the family and I gave one of the eulogies. I had very little time to prepare and decided to tell stories of their unlimited generosity. One story gave an account of the summer we were flooded out of our farm home.

Our whole California family had gathered for the July 4th celebration when the banks of the Sioux River broke and the land began to flood. Judd called the night before from their vacation lake home and said to Phil, "Gossie, get the hell out of that farm house. The river is rising and by morning you'll be surrounded by water." Gossie was a name Judd attached to Phil in medical school. I believe the name came from an author of their anatomy textbook.

Phil admitted he had trouble taking advice and we spent the night watching the river rise around us—by morning the water was four feet deep and another call came from Judd. He was coming with two vehicles to pick us up and take us to their home in Mitchell. Our farm house was higher and still dry when all ten of us managed to get out on a high-riding flatbed pulled by our caretaker on a tractor to Judd's waiting van. Judd, with his usual wit, told us we could stay at their Mitchell home until September as they were enjoying their lake home. Fortunately the water went down and, within a week, we returned to the farm.

Another story is treasured as it occurred the last time we saw them. We were back in South Dakota in November, 1996, for an event in Sioux Falls and to see my mother who lived approximately 120 miles northwest of Mitchell—which was midway from Sioux Falls. The evening was dark and cold and we decided to call ahead and stop for a cup of coffee with Boots and Judd on the way home. As we approached the driveway, we noticed that Judd had opened the garage door, taken out all the vehicles from the garage and turned on the lights so we could drive directly to the back door. When we arrived, he was waiting out front.

I used this story as a metaphor in the eulogy saying that one day we would see them again and Judd would open the doors, turn on the lights and be waiting outside to greet us. Others picked up on the light metaphor and one man told us that he was a lineman with the telephone company and had helped Judd plant hundreds of trees on the family property. He told us that after hearing the eulogy he was going to erect a light pole at the rear of the church to warm up that corner and make it more welcoming. He would do this at his own expense and dedicate the light pole to Judd and Boots. This was just the beginning of an enormous outpouring of love and respect from the community.

Several mutual friends tried to make sense of the accident—including one young friend who was with the fishing party and had dived in the water to retrieve the bodies. Since the consensus was that the accident was due to pilot error and the pilot survived, there were naturally hard feelings—especially since the pilot was local. I expect there are those who will always wonder what really happened. Phil and I will forever think that Judd could have crawled out the window and lived but courageously chose to risk his life to rescue Boots, although she is believed to have died instantly. Judd may have thought they could get out of the plane through a back door. He was so used to figuring things out, we could only imagine his anguish when the door didn't open and he knew he was going to die.

As for us, we stayed another day or two and helped where we could. At that point the children needed mostly to sleep and rest. We also planned to return to the farm in another few weeks and would see them all again. Phil suffered emotionally from all that was going on around him and felt helpless in his wheelchair. He often compared his reaction to the little boy in Rabbi Kushner's story from When Bad Things Happen to Good People. The Rabbi told of a little boy who had been sent on an errand by his mother. He was very late in returning and his mother was concerned. When he did come home, his mother asked why he was so late. He explained that his friend, Tommy, had wrecked his bicycle and was crying and he had stopped to help him. His mother questioned his motive and said, "You surely could not help with the bicycle." He replied that he could not help with the bicycle, but he had helped his friend cry. While I was busy with Paula and the many challenges she faced, Phil said all he could do was sit and cry. He lamented that he couldn't fix anything but maybe helped with the broken spirits. I am sure he did.

I have thought long and hard about this chapter in our lives. Through the years, we have stood by Boots's and Judd's children and watched their courage to live on with their families and their good works. Todd was married a few years later and I enjoyed officiating at their wedding. This is when I began to realize the power that comes from the courage of life—which is often less dramatic than a final moment but still holds a mixture of triumph and tragedy. At a time like this, a person does what he or she must do—in spite of the consequences or obstacles and often under pressure. Boots's and Judd's children had to decide for themselves the course they would follow. We could offer them comfort, hope and inspiration. But we could not supply courage itself. They had to look into their own souls and find the strength to meet their challenges. They chose to transform their loss and press on. This is the courage of life. And this is what they did.

A Prairie Star

The grace of God may step in when
you don't lose your head
in a clearly desperate situation

— *Carl G. Jung*

Not the usual farmer familiar to the Northern Plains, Uncle Ward Radcliffe was a Prairie Star—and I admired him. Intimate with the landscape, good to his neighbors and acquainted with grief and hard work, Uncle Ward left a noble legacy. His father, Amos Radcliffe, an immigrant from Liverpool, England, arrived in this country with a large group of Europeans in the late eighteen hundreds. Amos stayed a year or two in Ohio, married Ingle, and then set off for South Dakota where he homesteaded the family farm.

Uncle Ward was born on the farm in 1895 and died there in 1978. Educated mostly at home, he enjoyed reading books and also learned to play the piano, which his mother had brought from Ohio. In 1921, Ward married my mother's oldest sister, Myrtle. After a few years of farming on the homestead, the Great Depression hit the Plains and he and Myrtle, along with several cousins, moved to Lancaster, California, where they rented land and raised a family. At the beginning of World War II, however, Uncle Ward was ready to move back to South Dakota and to the homesteaded land, which he had inherited.

I was nine years old when they returned and excited to have my cousin Roseanne, who was my age, live closer to me. We became friends and often spent Sunday afternoons together. I enjoyed visiting their farm as Uncle Ward and I, through music, struck up our own relationship. He liked to hear me sing and he enjoyed playing the piano. This was unusual for a farmer in our area. I did not know any other farmers who had a piano, let alone could play one. Uncle Ward had long reddish fingers, which were discolored from a skin rash—I expect he had psoriasis. His fingers were also stiff from arthritis and hard work, yet, when he sat down on the three-legged black horsehair piano stool, his hands danced over the keys and his music radiated sheer delight. Playing mostly from memory or "by heart," as we used to say, he especially liked to recall church hymns and would invite me and Roseanne to sing with him. At the close of our musicale, akin to a benediction, we always sang "In the Garden"—his favorite hymn.

Although he was a successful steward of the land, I often wondered, then and later, if he really wanted to be a farmer, as he was a wonderful teacher and often stood in for the teachers in the nearby country school. His love for literature was obvious, as during our Sunday afternoon visits he would also read poetry. Not that other farmers didn't appreciate music and literature, but most of the men I knew were more inclined, on a Sunday afternoon, to clean guns, play cards, throw a game of horseshoes, go fishing or take a nap.

Along with the music and the literature, Uncle Ward had the demeanor of a gentleman. Perhaps it was his English genes, but his soft-spoken, civil tongue, was rare among the hard-working farmers. There was a dignity about him and even at my young age, I noticed an inner quietness, a calm composure—one that I would later recognize as a contemplative spirit. He would call my attention to the beauty of the prairie grasses, the sky, a bird song, or a wild rose growing in a ditch by the side of the road. He also consistently offered a table prayer before a meal, and always the same prayer. With bowed head and hands folded, he would reverently recite: "We beseech thee, Heavenly Father…"

Known for his generous spirit toward less fortunate farm families and needy relatives, others respected Uncle Ward for his good works and acts of mercy. He inspired me and I loved to converse with him in the "living room" of their modest farm house. I tried to absorb his simple, unpretentious wisdom. He encouraged me to study and read, go to college and find a life beyond the rural community. His thoughtful manner and kind words never leave me: "The world is changing," he said, "and you need to prepare for a different way of life."

After I finished college, except to visit my parents, I seldom returned to the farm community. I married, lived away from the area, travelled, engaged in new communities and enjoyed life with my husband and three children. I did make a point of sending Uncle Ward and family Christmas greetings and inquired about him from my mother. Roseanne and I attempted to keep in touch, but we were both busy with our families and close communicating was not possible. She married a fine young farmer with land and cattle and who eventually became the State Secretary of Agriculture. Uncle Ward was proud, but more for his immigrant father, Amos, and the respect for the years of struggle they had all endured as farmers on the Northern Plains. Shortly after this stunning family recognition, Uncle Ward died. Revered by all, he had led the way.

I was somewhat surprised to hear Roseanne's voice on the phone, asking if I could possibly attend the funeral, as Uncle Ward had requested that I sing a hymn at his memorial service. At that time, we lived approximately three hours (driving time) from the small town of Wessington and the church in which I had grown up and been married. I hesitated as it was December and the snow and ice had come, making the roads unpredictable. Fortunately, on December 10th that year, the weather report indicated a warming trend and the roads were believed to be clear. Due to previous commitments, I made the decision to drive up and back the same day. The service was scheduled for 11:00 and I was confident that by leaving at 7:00 a.m. I would be there in good time for the service. I really did not need to rehearse as the organist, Mary Chesbro, had accompanied me many times during my growing-up years. We would make contact, hum a stanza or two and know we would be fine with the old familiar hymn, "I Come to The Garden," as requested by Uncle Ward.

On that chilly December morning, I awakened early. Phil left for surgery and I said goodbye to the children at the breakfast table. As I was leaving a friend came to see the family out the door to school and turn off the lights. The air was crisp and clear and the street lights were coming on. With very little traffic, I was on the edge of town in fifteen minutes and in position to turn onto the major highway leading west to my hometown. As I went under the first large viaduct, I noticed the semi-trucks were driving at an unusually slow speed. I passed one and proceeded down the highway and came upon another one traveling at an even slower speed. I could not understand why, as the road looked clear of snow and by this time there was plenty of light. As I started to pass the second big truck, I felt the car begin to glide. It was then that I noticed the black ice on the road. I kept going beyond the truck and then the car began to spin. Fortunately, the spin of three turns took me to the ditch on the opposite side of the truck and I landed in a huge snowdrift. Neither of the trucks stopped—can't say that I blamed them as they no doubt were afraid to use the brakes. I pushed the door open in the snow and realized I was stuck with no way of getting out on my own. This was before car phones—at least I didn't have one—or any kind of a device to connect with anyone. I wasn't cold, in fact, the sun was beginning to shine and I noticed it was a beautiful morning, but what was I going to do? I looked up and down the road, and could see no cars, when suddenly from out of nowhere came a tow truck!! Do you think the truckers radioed back for help? I have always thought so. The jolly driver got out and said, "Hey, are you OK? You are really stuck... want some help?" I said, "How did you know?" By this time, he was hooking on a chain and roaring his engine. He didn't hear my question. Within a few minutes he had pulled my car back on the highway. All I had was a twenty dollar bill, which I gave him. I said, "I wish I had more." He replied, "Oh, that's more than enough, I am lucky if I get five bucks from most people." He drove off and I drove on down the road.

The traffic had increased and was moving at normal speed now—the morning sun had cleared the ice. With two and a half hours to go, I picked up a little speed and arrived at the familiar small town church by 10:40. My mother was obviously nervous and my friend at the organ was preparing someone else to sing, but I made it. I ran to the bathroom in the basement—which seemed like a mile away—brushed my hair, and, within a few minutes, dashed back up the basement stairs, ducked past the mourners, nodded at Roseanne, and made my way to the front of the church. Glancing over the congregation, I took a deep breath and suddenly felt a calm composure move through me. I was standing beside Uncle Ward at the old farm piano, I could see his red raw fingers touching the keys, playing the introduction to the hymn, and I began to sing, "I come to the garden alone, while the dew is still on the roses, and the voice I hear falling on my ear, the Son of God discloses, and He walks with me, and He talks with me..."

I often think of the truckers—so long ago—who showed mercy on me that December morning. I am convinced they guided their trucks on the ice away from my car, which kept me safe, and called for help. Because of them, I was able to sing and offer my benediction to Uncle Ward—a Prairie Star.

One Good Teacher

Wow, what a ride!

— Geraldine Chesley

After eight years of attending a one-room county school house, I was excited to enter high school, which was located in the small town of Wessington, South Dakota, seven miles from our family farm. Typical of small towns on the Northern Plains, all grades, K-12, were housed in one three-story school building. Lower grades occupied the first floor and upper grades the second and third floors. In 1946, there were 83 high school students from town and country and 23 in my freshman class—with 12 of us coming from one-room country schools. I knew most of those in my class as we had all been part of the small town community.

Instead of riding a horse, as I did to the country school, I rode with my brother, Vince, in a black 1940 second–hand Plymouth car. During my junior year, after Vince graduated, I drove the car alone during the fair weather months and boarded with friends in town during the winter months. The old black Plymouth worked very well with the exception of the doors, which had a tendency to fling open while turning a corner or, once shut, were difficult to re-open. Upon arrival at school and to avoid being tardy, I often had to climb out the window. After school and with the help of my old friends, the neighborhood boys, I would push and shove and finally get the door open.

The car became something of a school joke and upon arrival at the school parking lot, I learned to expect an audience looking out the assembly hall window. I imagined my classmates saying, "Will she climb or won't she climb?" One day after school, I drove my friends downtown only to have all four car doors swing open as I turned the corner on Main Street. Little did I know that my mother was coming to town that afternoon and there she was, standing on the corner with her friends. She looked both terrified and appalled, but when we all waved and laughed, she smiled, as she understood the problem of the doors.

For a town of 300 residents, and a long way from anywhere, the School Board hired qualified teachers and I vaguely recall several of them, but the memory of Geraldine Chesley brightly lingers. She taught English literature my junior and senior year. Thoughts of her are as vivid today as they were 70 years ago: A short, chubby lady with a jolly persona, Miss Chesley entered the classroom radiating joy and enthusiasm. She also daily carried a stack of books up to her chin and set them on her desk. So as not to distract her, we all held our breath and "chilled out" when we saw her coming with the books tucked under her chin. As she set the books on her desk, we would clap and she would laugh. Her face was very round and when she laughed, it turned beet red and her curly hair would swish over her sparkling eyes. Her laughter—which was really a giggle—amused us. Wearing floral print dresses, dark-rimmed glasses and black sturdy "nursing" shoes, she presented a vibrant scholarly presence. At first, a few of the boys tried to give her a hard time, but in the spirit of *Goodbye, Mr. Chips* or Robin Williams in the *Dead Poet Society,* Miss Chesley prevailed and won their respect as well as their hearts.

Over the summer, my brothers thought they had fixed the car doors and I started my senior year confident that the car-door problem was solved. However, one late October morning, as I drove into town, I passed the post office and saw Miss Chesley coming down the steps carrying her load of books. Overnight, the weather had turned chilly and I noticed she was not wearing a coat. I pulled up beside her, rolled down the window, and asked if she would like a ride. With a sigh of relief, she said, "Yes, please… " I went around to the passenger side and held her books while she climbed into the car. After stacking the books to her liking, I returned to the driver's seat and proceeded to drive. We chatted about the weather and then came to the corner leading to the schoolhouse. Fortunately, I was driving slowly as I turned but the doors all flew open. Out went Miss Chesley's books and out went Miss Chesley—at least most of the way out. She grabbed the door and was hanging on with one shoe on the ground. Her face was red and her curly hair on end, but her wonderful round body saved her from falling as she was stuck between the seat and the door. I was terrified until I heard her famous giggle followed by "Wow, what a ride!" I stopped the car and ran around to help her. I said, "Oh, Miss Chesley, I am so sorry." She replied, "Oh, never mind, I like a bit of adventure." Then, I picked up her shoe and glasses, gathered her books, which she looked over carefully, and we drove on to school. Thank heavens, as the car stopped, the door opened and she marched into the building as if nothing had happened. By the time I gathered my composure, she was already in the classroom and the books were on her desk. I reluctantly entered the room only to hear a resounding applause. Little did I know that my classmates had looked out the window and witnessed the whole scenario.

I graduated the following spring and Miss Chesley helped me write my graduation speech. She also reviewed my college applications, as I was the only student planning to attend a university. Above all, Miss Chesley let me know that she believed in me. She thought I could do anything I wanted to do... but she hoped I would further my education and continue to read creditable literature. Her deep commitment to the value of education left a lasting impression on me. I still have the poetry books she gave me.

Everyone needs one good teacher. I had mine.

Blowing in the Wind

May joy and peace surround you,
Contentment latch your door,
And happiness be with you
And bless you evermore.

— *An Irish Blessing*

Memories of the warm October evening linger. Earlier in the day Phil and I had gone to the farm to finish garden work and store the gladioli bulbs for winter. I had prepared a picnic supper and we were starting for the house when an ominous gust of wind blew through the farmyard. I said to Phil, "What was that?" He replied, "I don't know, it was strange and came up quickly." As we entered the house, I paused and said, "I wonder if we should go back to town, I feel a little anxious." Phil said, "Why don't we." I checked the house, picked up the basket of food, called the dog to jump in the pick-up and we started the forty mile drive back to town.

The sun was setting and the October day was turning to twilight. Golden fields left from harvest dotted the landscape alongside the corn fields still standing, waiting to be picked. This was our favorite season in the Dakotas. As I recall, we did not say much on the drive back, except to mention the beauty of the fields and sky and the warm October air. I also noticed that Phil was driving a little faster than usual. We both sensed a need to get to our home in Sioux Falls where we lived and worked. The farm was our place to linger and enjoy the gardens and all the wonders of being in the country—but that evening we hurried away.

We were in the house no more than ten minutes when the phone rang. Aunt Mildred's voice came on. "Hello, Jo. Is Phil there too?" I said, "Yes, Aunt Mildred, what is it, I will call him." Phil picked up another phone and Aunt Mildred's voice broke as she said, "Bill is dead in the upstairs bedroom—what should I do?" Phil expressed our sorrow and gently told her to call the coroner and we would try to drive over as soon as possible and help with the arrangements.

Uncle Bill and Aunt Mildred lived two hours away from us. He was Phil's mother's brother and a dentist in a small town near an Indian reservation. We were their surrogate children. Through the years they came for all the family gatherings. Aunt Mildred was delightful and brought cheer and energy to the family circle. She was known for her chocolate cake, albeit most of the family did not credit her for making the cake—but I did. She loved beauty, bling and bluster, and I welcomed her refreshing contributions, as she offered contrast to the

Germanic personalities around the table. Dressed with a flair for color and strong perfume, I smiled to feel the room rock when she entered. Mildred had one sister, Grace, an actress, living in New York City and married to a Hall of Fame athlete with a high profile in the New York Athletic Club. They also had no children. The sisters wrote daily to one another and used scented envelopes. Mildred also wrote to me. Our mailman would bring one of her letters and say, "Here is a letter from Aunt Mildred—I smell the perfume." She loved New York City and lived for her yearly visit to her sister. Uncle Bill never wanted to go or maybe he knew he could never keep up with Mildred and stayed home to rest. He enjoyed taking care of his Indian patients and was known as a kind, gentle man.

Phil asked Aunt Mildred details regarding the burial, assuming the service would be in the town where they had lived for sixty years. She replied, "Oh, no, we want to be buried near you and we want Jo to plan the memorial service." I recall Phil looking at me with a slight twinkle in his eye and saying, "Do we know where we are going to be buried?"

The next day, Phil went back to work and I went to the cemetery and bought five cemetery lots – two for them and three for us as our youngest son was only nine. Then I called a Lutheran minister friend, as Uncle Bill was Lutheran, and we organized a service. A week later, friends provided food and relatives gathered at our home before the funeral. Grace and her husband arrived from New York and although a bit intimidated, I carried on and everything went well. Two days after Grace returned to New York she called and said she had never experienced a lovelier cemetery and would I please go buy two more cemetery lots. I will never forget the look on the face of the desk clerk when I told her why I had come.

Two years later, Aunt Mildred became ill and came to stay with us. Within a few months, she died of cancer. Grace was a frequent visitor—always wearing a big hat and carrying a red rose as she stepped from the plane. I called my Catholic priest friend to offer Mildred's mass as she and Grace were Catholic. Grace and Dick stayed on after the funeral and cleaned out Mildred's house. Grace smiled in telling me all that she uncovered, including sixty-two hats in one room.

A few years after we moved to California, Grace called to tell us that Dick had died and asked if I would come to New York and give the eulogy. The service would be held at the Athletic Club. Phil wanted me to go so I composed a few thoughts, took out my black suit, and flew to New York. When I arrived at her apartment, Grace announced that she was not up to going to the service. I would represent her. I couldn't believe she would not go, as there were people coming from many distances to see her and honor her husband. I spoke to as many as possible, said she wasn't well, and extended her appreciation. But, alas, I was dumbfounded.

She requested that Dick's ashes be given to her and held until she died so they would be interred together. By mistake his ashes were sent to the cemetery in Sioux Falls and kept until she died several years later. It was against the rules of the cemetery to hold ashes, but the cemetery board agreed to keep them until Grace died. I made a few trips back to New York City, but I fear Grace died as a lonely old woman in a big city. By this time, Dick's ashes had sat on a shelf at the cemetery office in Sioux Falls for nearly four years. The following summer, Phil and I went back and, along with Msgr. James Doyle, officiated at the burial of their ashes. There were a few of Grace and Mildred's relatives at the cemetery and a few of our friends. Security guards were also placed on the grounds as there were rumors of contested money concerns among the relatives. I chose to ignore most of the discussion regarding the estate and don't know what happened to the money, but I believe most of it was left in New York City. As I left the cemetery and looked back at the four graves, I remembered the afternoon at the farm and the mysterious gust of wind, which to me marked the Alpha and Omega of these dear folks. I rejoiced to see them together at last.

EPILOGUE

To think of Mildred and Grace, I give thanks for their lives and their example of devotion and loyalty to one another. They grew up in a small prairie town, and had minimal education and little money. One stayed on the prairie, one went to New York City. They both married well and neither had children. I admired them for their courage to be their true selves. They believed in the value of beauty, goodness and mercy, discipline and duty. And in spite of their opposite life-styles and characteristics, they loved and edified each other. Memory of their radiant joy, sense of wonder and good company lingers.

An Interrupted Life

(Based on a true story.)

God grant me the serenity
to accept the things I cannot change;
the courage to change the things I can;
and the wisdom to know the difference.

— *Reinhold Niebuhr*

My name is Jeff and I was in love with Laura—a bright, beautiful, and happy medical student. In medical school, she was way ahead of me in smarts. Since I never had a girlfriend smarter than I imagined myself to be, I was a bit taken aback. She was also trustworthy, made friends easily and was kind to everyone. We planned to marry and had a date set for the wedding. Then, Laura was diagnosed with multiple sclerosis. She could barely walk and her speech blurred. My parents questioned the wisdom of going ahead with our plans. Laura said, "Jeff, I will always love you, but it isn't fair for you to be saddled with my poor health. We must call off our wedding." She urged me to finish medical school without her and go on with my life. I felt I had no choice. I did as Laura asked and finished my medical training. Later, I married a lovely woman and have two beautiful children. Yet, I cannot bring closure to my thoughts of Laura. The experience feels like an open wound. Questions haunt me: "Could I have helped her?" "Should we have talked more?" "Was it the right thing to do?" Once we said goodbye, she never contacted me again. She said, "It is better this way."

As I rationalize my feelings, thoughts of her cross my mind and I drift into a relentless melancholy. I hesitate to tell Emily, my wife, as I don't want to hurt her and I am not comfortable telling friends who might question my emotional intelligence. Instead, with hope that the process will bring needed healing and peace, I am moved to write of Laura's interrupted life and our relationship—what and how Laura and I met during our first year of medical school.

I was initially put off by her intellect and confident demeanor. Even though we took the same pre-med courses, she absorbed her studies easily while I, and our classmates, trailed behind. Fortunately, by the end of the first year, we all began to somewhat relax and Laura and I became good friends.

During our second year, we decided to study together and our relationship developed into a healthy romance. We liked to walk and talk, hold hands, go to an occasional movie and linger as we kissed each other goodnight. We felt privileged to be in medical school and shared our noblest desires to make good use of our careers. When she was beside me, I felt stronger and full of possibility. In the classroom, I would look across at her and know I wanted to be with her forever.

The following summer we took jobs apart and felt the pain of separation. We wrote letters and made phone calls, but did not see each other until August and the beginning of our third-year. Instead of classrooms, third year students were assigned to various clinical services. Laura and I did not draw the same services and missed being together during the day. Later in the evenings, we tried to meet but were usually so tired we could barely talk. Instead, we wrapped ourselves in each other's arms, and discovered our love and need for one another. As we looked forward to internship, the inevitable pain of separation again haunted us. We decided to get married the following spring before our senior year and would apply for a combined internship. To seal our plans, I gave Laura a ring for her birthday. Our families were thrilled and so were we.

Laura continued to be academically at the top of our class but I worried about her working too hard. She seemed tired and worn down. Not long after our engagement I noticed she began to walk with difficulty. She also expressed concern about blurring of vision. Together, we went to a neurologist to find out what was the matter. After a series of tests, she was given the presumptive diagnosis of multiple sclerosis. We were stunned. Even though the symptoms disappeared in a short while, Laura remained pessimistic about the prognosis.

Her energy was low and we knew her health was in jeopardy.

During Christmas break, we drove to Laura's home to make plans for our April wedding. By this time, Laura was struggling to walk and reached for a wall to balance. Her speech was slurred and she struggled with fatigue. Alarmed and bereft, her mother suggested we visit with a family friend who had multiple sclerosis. The friend, an orthopedic surgeon, was diagnosed during his senior year of residency. At the time we met him, twenty-five years after his diagnosis, he was enjoying a successful medical practice and participating in family and community activities. No doubt Laura's frightened mother was reaching for encouragement and trusted her friend would listen and advise.

The memory of that evening visit lingers. A light snow had fallen and the old English Tudor home of Dr. and Mrs. Gross looked like something out of a fairy tale. Everything seemed surreal. Dr. Gross met us at the door and Mrs. Gross ushered us to a sofa by the wood-burning fireplace. After chatting about medical school, icy roads, how well the birch wood burned and how the aroma filtered outside into the cold December evening, we settled down to talk.

Dr. Gross explained his experience with the disease and his good fortune in being able to live a reasonably normal life. Although he tried to assure us that this course of action was possible for Laura, he also cautioned that the diagnosis and the progression of the disease affects people differently. Laura listened closely to the conversation, nodded her head, smiled and appeared relaxed until suddenly her mood changed. She looked directly at Mrs. Gross and said, "Do you think we should go ahead with our plans for the wedding?" I sat quietly, feeling the pain in her question. Mrs. Gross responded appropriately by saying, "Only the two of you know how to answer that question. Phil and I had been married six years and had a two-year-old daughter when he was given the diagnosis. Your circumstances are different." As we thanked them and stood to leave, they both reached out and embraced us. Mrs. Gross said, "We will think of you." They walked us to the door and we went out into the cold winter night.

Urged by our concerned parents, we put the wedding plans on hold and returned to school. By February, Laura began to have more problems. We cancelled the wedding. Laura struggled to finish her clinical services, but by the end of the semester she was not able to continue. She would use the summer for rest and possible rehabilitation. I returned to my old job, and, when possible, drove to see her. Her progress was slow and by summer's end, we knew she would not return to medical school.

I entered my final year without her and felt my whole world had collapsed. We kept in touch by phone but I was not free to see her for several months. I could tell by her voice that her energy level had dropped. While I sensed she was discouraged, she never complained, only asked me about school, our classmates and my well-being. She hoped I would visit over the Thanksgiving holiday as she felt we needed to talk. By then, I was certain our marriage plans were over, but I was desperate to see her.

I drove to her home and was surprised not to find her there. Her distraught mother explained that earlier in the week, Laura had fallen again and she could not lift her. With regard for her mother's health, Laura asked to be admitted to a nursing home. This decision was consistent with her attitude of not wanting to be a burden on her family or me. I went to the nursing home and found her in a wheel chair reading a book. She looked up and gave me her beautiful smile. I kissed her and sat down with her hand in mine. With a long loving look at each other, we began to talk. Laura wanted to know everything about school. I told her the events of the final days of the semester and the anxiety and stress surrounding the examinations. When I told her my studies had gone well and I had received my desired match to start an internship in July, she nodded and smiled again. Then her eyes filled with tears, as did mine, and she quietly said, "Jeff, our life together is over. I want you to take back the ring as I am in no shape to marry you, I would only be a burden." I tried to explain to her that being in the medical profession, I would have access to care for her and we could still enjoy our life together. However, she would hear none of this and took off the ring and gently placed it in my hand.

With noticeable effort, she went on to say that life in the home was challenging. She was trying to adjust, as she understood this was the only place for her now. She murmured that even if she felt diminished, the caregivers were kind and handled her transfers from wheelchair to bed very carefully. With a heavy sigh she said, "So please forget about me and go on with your life." I felt weak and sick to my stomach and tried to dispute what she was saying, but to no avail. Finally, I offered a compromise: would she please keep the ring, move it from her ring finger to her middle finger and wear it in memory of our love? Laura agreed to my request but emphasized the need to stop all communication.

During the ensuing months, I refused to take her last words seriously and frequently tried to telephone. She would not take my calls or answer my letters. A phone call to her mother told me that Laura was writing poetry, reading and reaching out to other patients. Her simple acts of kindness and her radiant smile were making a difference to those around her and helping her to handle her own sadness. Her parents purchased a van and took her to church, concerts and other community events, but her situation continued to deteriorate. Before long, she stopped going out, as staying in the nursing home was easier for everyone. Visitors came often and the staff reported astonishment at Laura's positive attitude and irresistible smile.

Time moved on for me as well. During the next dozen years, I moved to another state, developed my medical practice and enjoyed my marriage and family. Life continues to be good and all seemed well until a recent afternoon when Laura's mother called and said, "Jeff, I thought you would want to know Laura died this morning." Something snapped. I let out a gasp. Old questions came hounding back: *"Did I do the right thing by her?" "Should I have relented that last night in the nursing home?" Could I have made a difference in her life?"* Her mother, tearfully trying to explain and comfort, said Laura often spoke of me and a few days before she died removed the ring from her middle finger to her ring finger. She requested upon her death that her mother call me with the words: "Tell him, we did the right thing."

Now that the story is written, I feel better and realize I do not need to forget Laura. She is a part of me and what happened between us matters. Peace comes when I realize she never stopped loving me and even if she died with a broken heart, I choose to believe she forgave me. The satisfaction of knowing I did what she asked me to do inspires me to forgive myself. I may always wonder if I could have helped her—even if my medical knowledge tells me differently. I also find it remarkable that when I am with my family I feel her blessing. And, as I take care of patients and advance in my profession, I remember her. I deeply love my wife and the life we share. Laura would not want it any other way. And, I will continue to live with a thankful heart along with the memory of a former love disrupted by a dreadful disease. If I were given one wish it would to be to help find a cure for multiple sclerosis. There are too many young lives interrupted from this disease, too many hearts are broken and too many dreams are shattered.

Grief — Grace — and Goodness

Whoever survives a test, whatever it may be,
must tell the story. That is his/her duty.

— *Eli Wiesel*

As a result of the 2006 New Year's Eve flood in Ross, California, we were living in an apartment while our home on Shady Lane was being reconstructed. Similar to the previous three months, the spring rain kept coming. By this time, the amounts had reached 300% of normal with the chance of more flooding predicted. While driving, the relentless rain and blustery wind challenged my visibility and strength—especially with the large van which we had converted for Phil's access.

Margaret and Sophia, two of our granddaughters, ages 15 and 12, were with us for the weekend. There was a slight break in the weather Sunday afternoon and we decided to drop the girls off to visit their cousins, Athena and Gloria, while we attended a birthday party close by. After a happy, sunny afternoon, we started our drive to their home in San Francisco.

The rain and wind returned and I drove slowly with care as I felt some danger on the road. Phil was in his wheelchair in back with Margaret, and Sophia was in front with me. The wind was frightening as we crossed the Golden Gate Bridge and we distracted ourselves by chatting about the churning water in the Bay. As darkness approached, we arrived safely and parked in front of the apartment where the girls lived. They were glad to be home and made a dash for the door.

I went to the rear of the van to see if they had left anything behind. I lifted the van door and searched the area. The wind and rain persisted. Suddenly, without warning, the large hatchback van door came down and struck me in the right eye. Possibly due to the rain beating down, I did not see the door coming. From his wheelchair in the back of the van, Phil sensed something was wrong. I crawled in beside him and said, "The door hit my eye and I can't see." He noticed only a slight laceration and said, "Go in the house and have the girls put some ice on it. I'll be fine here." I fully suspected something more than a bump, but we began with the ice. We also called Cort, our oldest son, who lived fifteen minutes away. He came quickly and drove us to the closest emergency room. We were all stunned and I was certainly in shock.

After several examinations I was referred to the senior staff surgeon who asked that I be prepared for surgery. It was now midnight. Phil and Cort sat beside me. Dazed, with no pain, my whole face was numb. I recall being terribly cold and kind nurses wrapping me in warm blankets. After being wheeled toward the operating room, I asked Cort to pray. I faintly remember him standing over the hospital bed in the waiting area and whispering a prayer for mercy and the surgeon's competence. I often wondered what Phil felt at that moment. He was a stranger in familiar territory. For over thirty-five years and over thousands of patients he had been the surgeon, prepared and waiting to proceed. He would have known all the doctors and nurses in the room and they would have known him. He was a beloved surgeon but that day he was a husband in a wheelchair. Never had we felt our anonymity as poignantly. Wheeled further into the operating room, I waved good-by to him and my heart hurt to faintly see the dreadful look of despair on his face. He knew so much more than I did and feared the outcome.

Later I was told the surgical procedure took approximately two hours and when the staff surgeon came to see him, Phil was full of questions. They told him the surgeons had repaired a 14 millimeter (3/4 inch) laceration of the globe from which the retina had escaped. When Phil asked, "What can I do to help?" the primary surgeon answered, "Give her psychological support." No one would say whether I would be able to see with the eye again.

Phil slept on a cot beside me that night and the next morning I was discharged to the care of Dr. Campbell, my ophthalmologist in Marin. Again, there was no comment as to the loss of vision in the eye. Dr. Campbell was very gracious and concerned but demurred on my care and referred me to Dr. McDonald, a retina specialist. Dr. Campbell went to great lengths to explain how fortunate we were to have such a renowned specialist in the area. He also seemed upset when queried about the prognosis of the eye and left the room rather abruptly.

After all the build-up and recommendations of Dr. McDonald, Phil said he expected the renowned specialist to arrive as a knight in shining armor. Instead, Phil described "a handsome man with an immaculate appearance and a commanding professional manner. His tall, striking physique was complimented by a white shirt, pink bow tie, sharp-creased trousers and brilliantly shined loafers. There was enough gray at the temples to give him that look of distinction." After quickly dispensing with the introductions, Dr. McDonald examined the exterior of my injured right eye. He then covered my left eye and shone a bright light into the right eye. Each time, he asked: "Do you see any light?" And each time I said, "No." He had previously seen the operative note and was aware of the damage the eye had sustained. When he finished the exam, he must also have been aware of our unanswered questions as he quietly stepped back before he began to speak: "We all have one head, and one heart. But we have two eyes and you just lost one of them. Put these drops in both eyes and I will see you again in two weeks." With those words, Dr. McDonald left the room and the two of us looked at each other not knowing what to say or do. Our feelings were mixed between sadness, anger, disbelief and grief, and all of these emotions would be expressed in the coming days.

The first thing I noticed was my inability to judge distance. This was evident a few days later when we stopped at a local café for lunch. I had ordered tea and when I attempted to pour it from the pot to the cup, the tea went all over the table. Lesson #1: "When pouring things, use both hands and engage the spout on the lip of the cup before pouring."

We still had three or four months before the construction on our home would be completed so we decided simply "to make the best of it" and use the time wisely to learn how to live with one eye. Mounds of cards and letters, food and support arrived daily at our doorstep. A psychiatrist friend came by and pointed out that the eye, with its direct connection to the brain, is so much a part of the whole person that its loss is much different from losing an arm or a leg. I found this illuminating. From near and far, great wisdom, love and compassion poured over us. How could I not find courage to cope? Lesson #2: Be grateful. And, I was.

That is not to say there were no tears, or grief, or frustration. I remember one occasion when Phil was helping put drops in my eye, and as he stood up from his wheelchair he lost his balance and bumped my eye. I was having severe headaches and the eye was very tender. I let out a scream, ran to the bedroom and yelled, "You hurt me!" Phil heard me crying and came in to the bedroom. We sat there and cried together. It all seemed so unbelievable. We were both trying to be brave, and the reality seemed so brutal. Lesson #3: Be gentle with ourselves.

During the next few weeks, we learned from various sources that monocular vision is not uncommon. Many people have gone through life with sight in only one eye. The following are a few famous names: Theodore Roosevelt, Wiley Post, Sammy Davis, Jr. and Letty Russel, a renowned author/professor at Yale Divinity School. Letty learned of my accident from a mutual friend and called me from New Haven. Her empathy and caring concern inspired me—especially when she told me she had written three books and taught another ten years after the loss of her eye. Phil was fascinated with more research and studied monocular vision in birds and fish. Although we rarely think of this, the eyes of fish and birds are on the sides of their heads rather than the front. When a bird turns its head from side to side, the bird is focusing on one vision, then another, etcetera, to establish a location. From this, I learned why birds so often fly into a window: they can't see straight ahead. Lesson #4: Notice and keep learning.

After a second visit with Dr. McDonald, he referred us to a world-renowned ocularist in Oakland. Dr. McDonald told us that patients across the continent and the oceans come to this specialist who makes prosthetic eyes. He said, "I could send you to Tokyo or London but Steve Young is in our back yard and is the best in the world." I was a bit overwhelmed at hearing this generous referral from Dr. McDonald who uses words sparingly.

In late June of 2006, I began my life-changing experience with Steve Young—who preferred to be called "Steve," not "Doctor." I have never met anyone like him and probably never will. We entered his very plain office on the top floor of a tall unattractive building in Oakland. The office was stripped of the sterility and imposing stature of many doctors' offices. His wife, Renee, was the receptionist and the two of them administered the medical practice seven days a week, except on special holidays. We could quickly see why they were on the top floor of a tall building, as light poured in from three huge windows wrapped around the space. Obviously, the use of good light for painting the eyes is essential. During the first hour of our first visit, the ocularist determined that the eye was ready for the prosthesis and proceeded to take an impression. I was then excused and told to return in two hours and he would place the temporary prosthesis, made of thick clear plastic, into the eye. We followed instructions and returned later. At that time, Steve placed the prosthesis in the socket and told me to wear it for three weeks. In late July, I was scheduled to return for a three-day process and the final fitting of the finished eye.

As I mentioned, the office was unimposing, with six chairs in the waiting room next to a small office for Renee. There were two examining and treatment rooms with a small laboratory in between. Steve Young was as different as his office. He was a big man, probably 250 pounds, with a wild Einstein haircut going in all directions. His face was unusually round with large eyes and bushy eyebrows. He was always taking a break and he loved to eat salami sandwiches and pickles. With his easy manner and a constant friendly chatter—even while painting—he made us feel comfortable. I wondered if he had developed this rather bizarre manner to distract the patient from what was really happening. There was certainly no space for anxiety. To look at his stubby fingers, I could only wonder how he could paint the delicate iris and other parts of the eye. It was hard to imagine this man attracting patients from all over the world. Or was it? He was absolutely authentic and showed his caring concern for everyone who came through his door. His office walls were covered with photos from Saudi Arabia, Egypt, Europe and parts of Asia and Afghanistan. The latter photos were from eye injuries suffered during the war. Although both Dr. McDonald and Steve Young were internationally known, the contrast of their appearances and demeanors could not have been more opposite.

We asked Steve how he got into this particular phase of medicine. He explained that he was at the University of Iowa, either starting medical school or assorted work, when he became involved with the ophthalmology department. They were building a display and as he had an interest in art, he helped them with the artistic aspects. The professor in charge recognized his artistic talent and suggested that he become an ocularist, a relatively new department and specialty. This was in the early seventies. For a farm boy who grew up near Mason City, this was a stretch. His work soon gained national attention and he was lured to California by a prominent ophthalmologist in the Bay Area.

Phil kept reading and learning and told me that it was the dental technicians who came up with the idea of custom-fit eye prostheses. Prior to 1942, all the eyes were made by glass blowers in Germany. Although the eyes came in different sizes, they were not custom made. At that particular time, the Germans took a dim view of the Americans, and, due to the war effort, soon stopped their production. The dentists came to the rescue with an epoxy acrylic material. This was similar to the material used later to cement hip and knee replacements.

Steve sent me back for a final assessment from Dr. McDonald before he started the final steps toward completion. As predicted, Dr. McDonald swiftly entered the room, examined the eye and told me to return in six months. He then turned to leave as quickly as he had come. Halfway out the door, the elegant doctor turned around and sat down in a chair beside me. He took my hand and looked directly at me. In a warm and personal manner, dropping the professional façade, he said, "You know, Joan, if I could have saved your eye, I would have." I was deeply moved by his sincerity and caring regard— and I believed him. I uttered a weak "thank you" and he quietly—and slowly—left the room.

As scheduled, we returned for our three-day appointment with Steve Young in late July. Phil wanted to observe the entire procedure but could not get his wheelchair into the small office. When Steve stood in the doorway, even though he was only 5 feet 10, he filled the frame. He saw the problem and motioned to Renee. Together they handled the wheelchair and helped Phil hold on to the wall until we could move the chair toward him. We were humbled by their hands-on willingness to engage with us. What they do and how they do it is an incredible two-person show.

To paint the eye, Steve had a palette next to him with primary colors from which he mixed and mated using the other eye as a guide. His stubby fingers and camel hair brush did wonders. He explained that they had tried all sorts of computer-assisted techniques but none was as good as the human eye. He was intent on keeping us at ease and told a string of jokes to keep us amused. A small television was turned on over his shoulder. Occasionally, he would glance around and look for a few minutes, then return to his artistry. We went back for the final fitting the next day. After making our way through the door again, Steve went into the laboratory to retrieve the eye from the baking process. He then assisted me in placing the eye. When I looked at Phil, he caught his breath and with tears in his eyes looked up, smiled, and said, "You're back."

As we were leaving the office, Steve went into his makeshift kitchen and came out with a salami sandwich in one hand and a dill pickle in the other. He looked at Phil and said, "Here, Phil, take this, I think you need it more than I do." Lesson #5: Love everybody, as it takes all kinds of folks to serve humanity."

Phil loved to tell this whole story and would always end by saying: "Jo was over-the-top joyful with her new eye, she felt whole again, and my emotions were assuaged with a mouth full of salami."

EPILOGUE

I am writing this account in 2018. Twelve years have passed since that awful moment when the van door came down. The girls have grown up, Phil is gone, and life has moved on. I go back to see Steve and Renee every two years and in 2013 had a new eye made. While it is true that from the beginning, the adjustment was and continues to be challenging, yet I am grateful for all the people who carried me through the experience: The surgeons whom I never met at California Pacific Hospital, Dr. McDonald, Steve and Renee, friends and family who so deeply cared and, of course, Phil and his steadfast love that held us together through the flood, rebuilding of our home and all the circumstances surrounding the loss of the eye, all of which was happening at the same time. Unlike Letty Russel, I haven't written three books or taught ten years since the accident, but I have lived and loved and believed that all is well, and will be well, no matter. Above all, I have felt the tender amazing grace of God's presence.

Tending the Flame

Remembering My Mother

This story is adapted from my book, <u>Sunrise</u>. It is included in this section on "lives I carry with me," as my mother's strength of character abides. The hymn leading into the story was her favorite. I still hear her singing it.

Lead, Kindly Light,
amid the encircling gloom,
lead thou me on.

— John H. Newman

Affectionately regarded as the centerpiece of home life, the wood-burning kitchen range or stove—as the signature appliance was usually called—took on a mysteriously human quality. As a young girl growing up on the farm, I regarded the stove as part of the family— with a personality. Designed for wood, warmth and wonder, the wood-burning kitchen range was my mother's domain. She kept the wood burning all day and as the smoke escaped through a large stove pipe pushed through a hole in the roof, she sent a watchword. As if to comfort and cosset, the aromatic smoke from the burning wood created a plume over the farm yard and signaled a numinous message of peace.

While preparing daily meals was the main purpose of the kitchen range, Dad and Mother filled large boilers of water to heat on the stove for wash day and weekly baths. In summer, during canning season, water was boiled and used for preserving fruits and garden vegetables. Jams and jellies were also preserved by boiling the fruit on top of the stove. In autumn, after butchering, the back burners were kept warm for the rendering of lard. Mother also baked her classic fruit pies, bread, cinnamon rolls, cookies and angel food cakes in its oven. How she did this all alone—as well as working in the garden and taking care of chickens and children—will forever remain a mystery to me.

What went on over the top of the stove was usually handled by the adults in the family, but the massive oven door attracted the children. During the severe winter ice storms, one of my richest memories is helping my brothers gather small half-frozen farm animals—baby lambs, chickens and kittens—and placing them on the oven door to thaw. And yes, I do remember one time when the chickens thawed and flew through the kitchen. We also thawed frozen gloves, mittens, caps and boots. At night, we put our pajamas on the door to warm and on Saturday afternoon we warmed towels for the weekly baths.

Monday wash day was also carried out by the use of the stove. Early in the morning, Dad lifted the heavy washtubs filled with water from the well onto the stove. As the water heated, Dad moved the wringer washing machine out of the storage room, connected it to a generator and placed it next to the stove to access the water. He then left to feed the animals while Mother sorted the clothes. All this took place before breakfast while I was still in bed.

After Dad finished working with the animals and Mother had one load of wash turning in the hand-wringer machine, she fixed breakfast, which consisted of bacon and eggs plus homemade biscuits and jam—Dad's favorite. She also made beef stew early on wash day as the meat could cook on the back burner of the stove, behind the wash tubs, and was ready to eat at noon—the customary time for the larger meal of the day. Most of the year, the clothes were hung outside on a wire clothesline. During inclement weather, wooden racks were pulled into the kitchen and elsewhere around the house. Ironing was done with flat irons which were heated on the stove top. Mother would pick up one hot iron, attaching the handle to the groove on top, and proceed to iron a few pieces of clothing. When the iron cooled, she reached for another. For several hours, and often spread over a few days, she went back and forth to the stove, picking up a heated iron and placing another on the stove to reheat until the ironing basket was empty.

All this changed after World War II and to keep up

with the times we purchased a bottle gas stove. This was shortly before electricity, running water and inside plumbing came to the farms. A new era began. I recall what a great day it was when we exchanged the old black wood-burning stove for a gleaming white bottle gas stove. Our shiny gas stove had four burners and an oven with storage. No longer did we need to haul wood and corncobs or carry out ashes. All we had to do to keep the new stove functioning was to be certain the pilot light was burning. Great attention was given to one raw flame way down under the oven. Because the old farm houses had very little insulation and the floors were drafty, Dad wrapped black tar paper around the foundation and banked the house with straw bales. But no matter what he did, summer or winter, drafts would blow through the house and the draft coming through the kitchen would weaken or blow out the pilot light. I remember my mother tending the vulnerable flame. Kneeling, she would fan or blow on the flame, or strike a match, then stand back and wait until the flame started again.

At first the new stove was novel, easy to clean, and offered convenience. Yet we were bereft and homesick for the warmth and wonder surrounding the old kitchen range. Over time more changes came: electricity, plumbing, water heaters, automatic washing machines, home freezers, pressure cookers and more and more conveniences. We became accustomed to a new and easier way of life. But there was something so fundamental missing and we all felt it.

Through marriage, college, and other circumstances, the family changed as well. Eventually, Mother and Dad retired and moved to town. The hard physical work of the farm was over.

At certain times these childhood memories burn within me, especially the image of Mother on her knees keeping the flame alive. As if tending the holy, I eulogize her long-suffering work with the old kitchen range and am inspired by her steadfast resolve in tending the flame. The image continues to be a metaphor for all of life, teaching me the value of perseverance.

Tending the Holy

I want only to show you something I have seen

and to tell you something I have heard…

that here and there in the world and

now and then in ourselves

is a New Creation.

— *Adapted from Paul Tillich, The New Being*

Hold On To What Is Good

This homily was delivered in 2017 on Labor Day Sunday at First Presbyterian Church, San Anselmo, California.

We all have within us this capacity for wonder,
this ability to break the bonds of ordinary awareness
and sense that though our lives are fleeting and
transitory,
we are part of something larger, eternal and unchanging.

— *Philip Simmons*

Four years ago my family and I decided it was time for me to move into a retirement community. I recall thinking: *"How could I do this? How could I leave my home in this lovely neighborhood—and the street where I live? How could I leave my rose garden and my kitchen table? How could I leave a way of life that I cherished?"* I have often thought how life stories resemble books and how dramatic change and loss is akin to losing a bookmark. The narrative is altered. And so it was with me.

After I moved, I stumbled around a few months, wondering if I would ever fit into this new way of living. I sensed a loss of identity. Phil was gone, children scattered, and grandchildren who for over twenty-five years had run through my house were grown up and away. I imagined I was a bird with clipped wings. The need for purpose tormented me. *"Would I find purpose—Holy purpose—in this new reality?* Then, I felt a hand on my shoulder and a voice saying, "You are forgetting something. You have identity. You may feel changed but you are the same person you have always been. You need to hold on to what is good, believe in yourself and the life I gave you." I recognized the tender touch of the Holy Spirit. A favorite hymn echoed: "Breathe on me, breath of God, fill me with life anew, that I may will what thou would will and do what thou would do." I picked up my imaginary book, found my place, and re-engaged with my story. I would savor the memories and cease my relentless lament for all I missed. I would press on, as I knew if I stood still, I would turn to stone.

I began by looking around at the people who live where I live. I listened to their stories and found new appreciation for who they are. I experienced different belief systems and different backgrounds. Slowly, and with the help of friends and family, I regained confidence in who I am now and became aware of the many gifts of divine love and grace that sustain me. I recalled stories from living in third world countries where we learned that in cross-cultural situations, the key to ministry is to become the message. I thought of St. Francis saying, "Preach the Gospel always, sometimes use words." And of Maya Angelou who said, "People will forget what you said, people will forget what you did, but people will never forget how you made them feel."

These thoughts also remind me of the years I directed a soup kitchen. Is there really any difference? Doesn't the entire world need a soup kitchen? No matter where we work or live, how old or how young, with disadvantaged or advantaged people, our purpose—our holy purpose—is to celebrate life by being living reminders of the good news of God's grace. This is the story you have heard from all of us this morning—and it is your story too—the message we carry within us—the one we become. So onward with love and may God's Goodness and Mercy go with us all.

The Bread Connection

This homily was given May 6, 2018, at First Presbyterian Church, San Anselmo, California. The service was in celebration and closing of the Shelter Program.

Do this in remembrance of me...

— Luke 22:19

Early in my work of developing soup kitchens and shelters I recall a saying that never leaves me: When a person dreams alone, it is only a dream. But when we all dream together, it becomes a reality. This is the story of the shelter program.

In the fall of 2009, the Duncan Hall kitchen was being painted but was not in full operation and we had only two weeks to get ready. The dishwasher needed repair, we couldn't find all the silverware and we were short of glasses. We were also asked to serve two nights, back to back, that first year and hosted two neighboring churches who wanted to use our kitchen. My phone was busy as I had not advanced to computer planning. What I mostly remember is the magnificent response from the community and the joy we felt from the aroma of nutritious food and the satisfaction of meaningful hospitality. As we prayed together and opened our doors to welcome the homeless strangers that first night, we poignantly felt the presence of the Holy Spirit which stayed with us throughout the years.

Because I had visited several soup kitchens across the country where I felt the poor were mistreated, I admit to being intentional about not serving the poor poorly—a mantra of mine—and along with nutritious food I suggested we use tablecloths, cloth napkins and fresh flowers on the table. It was a stretch, but we did it. I felt vindicated when one evening one of homeless men stopped at the door and said, "I always feel I want to stand up straighter when I come here." Restoring dignity was one of our most powerful values.

The key to the program was the welcome table and the fellowship of eating together.

The act of sharing food and conversation initiates a different dynamic from the usual soup kitchens where food is dropped off. I often said that if Jesus were to come to our town on a Friday or Saturday night, he would want to eat with us and sleep on the floor with the other men.

Let me tell you of the epiphany—which illuminates my story and defines what I call The Bread Connection.

Approximately *thirty* years ago on the first Sunday of October I attended worship at the Cathedral of St. John the

Divine in New York City. I was in New York for the purpose of viewing soup kitchens and shelters in preparation for the work I was asked to do in my home state of South Dakota. I planned to meet my team the following day, but on this World Wide Communion Sunday, I wanted to worship with my family. To our surprise The Feast of St. Francis was also being observed and along with a crowd of worshipers, the cathedral was full of animals—all kinds of animals from monkeys to snakes—as well as an elephant, and a camel walking down the center aisle. The service included movements of dance, song and incense. It was a wild and wonderful celebration including Paul Winter on the soprano saxophone playing music from the St. Francis collection. But what really struck me was what happened as the priest lifted the bread for the Eucharist. From the balcony came a thundering drumroll and a blast of trumpets! I thought only in New York could this happen. Then, I thought, but why not? This was the table of our Lord reminding us of what he said, "Do this is remembrance of me." Jesus did not say, "Think this," or "Consider this," or "Pray about this." Jesus said, "Do this." He called for love in action.

With this in mind, the next day our group assembled and participated in a soup kitchen on the lower east side of Manhattan. In two hours 847 men came off the street and through the line to eat. I was asked to hand out bread as the men left the dining hall. As I held the bread box and watched the hundreds of hands reach in, I heard those words from the day before. A trumpet sounded inside of me and with every heartbeat, the drums began to roll. I knew that through this bread, I was intimately connected to the compassion of Jesus. This was his bread and the bread given to me at the cathedral was the same bread I was giving that day and the same bread broken in the programs that followed—including the shelter meal at our church and all the churches throughout the area. Through this bread connection "do so in remembrance of me" takes on a deeper meaning—especially as we serve the poor and disadvantaged.

The memory of lessons learned these past nine years will linger. Duncan Hall and the kitchen have received a permanent blessing and so has our community. In that sacred space we became aware that just because a person is poor or homeless and a bit torn and tattered doesn't mean he is less of a person. We learned that impoverished people really don't care how much you know until they know how much you care. And as we watched the children and young people come and go, our hearts felt a ring of hope that seeds of goodness and mercy were being planted. And as we worked together we learned to pray with our feet and hands. Words were not as necessary to the homeless men as was our presence to them and their presence to us—a mutuality of hosting and being hosted developed.

It was a holy time. It was communion. So let the trumpets sound and the drums roll as we move on, and may our hearts be filled with gratitude for the task we were given to do.

The Faithful Donkey

In quietness and confidence
shall be your strength.

— Isaiah 30:15

Palm Sunday

While not unusual to wonder what was at work in the mind of Jesus as he jogged along on the dusty trail toward Jerusalem, my thoughts take me to the faithful donkey that carried him. I imagine the donkey tied to a tree waiting on the outskirts of Jerusalem. I see his eyes as he patiently stands, occasionally shifting one leg with another. I see his tiny hooves and the rope tossed around his neck. I imagine drawing closer and smelling the sweat as I touch his dusty coat. I lay my head against his mane and whisper, "Do you know what is ahead for you?" Do I imagine him trembling? Does he sense his captured obedience, his significance? Then, I see him led away and mounted by a stranger. Under my breath, I murmur, *"Don't be afraid, little donkey—you are chosen to perform this task*."

What do we make of the faithful donkey? The scriptures tell us nothing about the burden or fatigue or difficulty or poor state of the road experienced by the donkey. As he takes that first step toward Jerusalem, he appears not to be thinking of himself, only of the stranger on his back and the dusty journey ahead. Yet in that first step, all was achieved.

If faithfulness is one of the sturdy qualities most dear to the heart of God, then the significance of the donkey plodding steadily forward is telling. Are we not called to accept common duty and challenging tasks? Without reference to our own desires, are we not asked to pick up our feet and steadily move forward, knowing that what we do bears witness according to God's will?

Beloved poet Mary Oliver wrote of the donkey, "I hope, finally, he felt brave. I hope, finally, he loved the man who rode so lightly upon him, as he lifted one dusty hoof and stepped, as he had to, forward."

To think of the donkey summons our humility and, yes, reminds us to be brave. As we walk the green paths of our little towns and countrysides, we will remember the dusty path taken by the donkey and plod onward with courage and faithfulness to fulfill our chosen purpose.

The River Jordan

"The Lone, Wild Bird in lofty flight
Is still with Thee,
nor leaves Thy sight.
And I am Thine, I rest in Thee.
Great Spirit come, and rest in me."

— Henry McFadyen

While on a trip to Israel in 1985, I was baptized in the River Jordan. The year before, and with a heavy heart, my mother told me that I had not been baptized. I sensed she felt some shame and embarrassment. She was getting older and asked if I would consider coming back to the country church of my childhood and receive the sacrament along with my sister and two brothers—who, like me, were all in their fifties. The Community Church of our childhood was not affiliated with a denomination until later when the church became under the aegis of the Presbyterians. It was at that time that Mother and her friends realized that their children had not been baptized. This knowledge became a burden to her and as she approached her eighty-eighth birthday, she decided to reveal her secret with the hope that I would right the wrong she imagined—which hung so heavy on her heart.

By this time, I had been engaged in years of service to the church—wherever I lived. The year I learned of this, we lived in Sioux Falls, South Dakota, where we had baptized and raised our children and been active in the community. We had recently returned from a six-month mission trip to Nepal, under the sponsorship of the Presbyterian Church, and we later represented South Dakota at the National Prayer Breakfast in Washington, D.C. Also, because I wanted to deepen my faith through study and an increased knowledge of the scriptures, I had enrolled in the local seminary.

The day my mother asked me to be baptized, I pondered the question and said to myself, *"Why? Why now? Was I missing something? What about my steadfast faith commitment that spanned my lifetime?"* I recall I mumbled something back to my mother that said I needed a little time to think about this. I knew I did not want to "go home again" and I found the thought of being baptized in the Sioux Falls church awkward—especially since I was an ordained elder and had taught the confirmation classes plus given dozens of programs to the women's groups. After a few weeks of trying to sort it out, I decided to delay the response.

A year passed and, in the meantime, we—Phil, Robert (now 14) and I—signed up for a tour of Israel with members of the seminary community. This was incorporated into the curriculum for those who wanted credit and the participants included several seminary professors. There were also students from a Catholic seminary and a diverse number of people who simply wanted the experience—by then we had a bus-load.

At this point I also needed time to consider a request from the Catholic Diocese: The Bishop wanted to develop a community program to feed the poor and disadvantaged of Sioux Falls, and he wanted me to be a part of "a handful of souls" that would work with him. Would I do this? Traveling through Israel seemed like the perfect time to examine all three questions—all of which hung heavy on my mind.

As we landed in Israel and began touring the countryside, the towns, and the holy sites, I recalled a song I had heard forty years before at the summer music camp where Phil and I had met. It was written and sung by Geoffrey O'Hare. The first line went like this: "I walked today where Jesus walked in days of long ago." As I journeyed through Israel, I found myself humming this tune.

Leaving Nazareth, we drove toward the River Jordan. The day was overcast and cool. Before us, as we stepped away from the bus and gathered by the river, I noticed two different groups of people in the water. They were wearing white robes and a ceremony was being performed. Clearly, this was a pilgrimage leading to a group baptism. I was mesmerized and as I came out of my trance, I glanced up at my friend, Tom Johnson, an ordained Presbyterian minister, who was sitting on a high rock above the river. I leaped toward him and said, "Tom, what would you think of baptizing me in the River Jordan?" I explained my circumstances and apologized for the outlandish request. He looked at me and I wasn't sure if he or the rock was about to fall into the river. Then, I heard him mumble, "Let me think about it." Later, we drove to a small Kirk of Scotland (the name of the original Presbyterian Church) for a worship service. While visiting with the pastor, Tom borrowed the Book of Order from the Kirk. The Book of Order is the official handbook that defines the sacraments and ceremonies of the church as well as the rules and regulations. Every Presbyterian Church around the world refers to this highly-regarded document.

At 6:30 the next morning, Tom knocked on our door and said, "We are turning the bus around and going back to the river for your baptism."

The plan was that we would wear our traveling clothes, take off our shoes and stockings and wade into the river—carrying the Book of Order. The diverse group of traveling companions would serve as my support community. Since the rocks on the floor of the river were slippery and there were hundreds of minnows swimming around our feet, Tom and I held on to each other and very gingerly went out about five feet into the water, but still on the shore of the river. The cool waves washed over our feet. I smile when I think of Tom saying to me, "Jo, if I slip and fall, don't worry about me but please rescue the

Book of Order." He then performed the simple ritual with dignity and depth. The group witnessing the ceremony was silent. All I could hear was the gentle sloshing of the river against the banks. After we climbed out of the river and joined the group, I quickly filled a bottle of river water for my mother. I wanted her to have this for the baptism of my sister and brothers. I finally had my response to her noble request.

I also heard the answer to the request from the Bishop. This came to me in the form of a call: As I beheld the diverse group standing by the river on my behalf, I saw the faces of hungry children and the anguished faces of the elderly. I heard the cries of the homeless and of the working poor and hungry, and I knew that their sorrow was my sorrow. I would accept the call and work with the Bishop.

I have often wondered what the others gathered by the river were thinking that morning. Were they also inspired? The serenity of the moment lingers, as does the quiet walk back to the bus. Only after a few miles down the road did we start to talk again.

Yes, I walked that day where Jesus walked, and stood in the river where he stood—and where he was baptized. The third question was answered: "Did baptism matter to me?" How could it not? The last line of the old song reads:

"And I felt him close to me."

Yes, everlastingly!

The Moon And Me

Through many dangers, toils and snares,
I have already come;
'Tis grace has brought me safe thus far,
and grace will lead me home.

— *John Newton, "Amazing Grace."*

I awakened early and was delighted to see a full moon off my patio window. I pulled up a chair, turned off the lights and with only the fireplace burning, watched the moon for as long as it stayed in the sky—full, bright, warm to the eyes, and beautiful. I could see the moon was moving slightly and I was fascinated by the light that glowed until it gently slipped into the darkness and disappeared. *How magnificent if life were like this,* I thought... *to stay whole, bright and aglow until we slip away.*

Alas, we know that being fully alive and well until the end is not the usual reality. We are mortal, and as we make choices and invest in what matters most in life, we acknowledge our vulnerability. And in so doing, we acknowledge the powerful connection between living well and dying well.

And, so, I ask myself: *What is it now that matters the most, what is it that keeps me living well?* I think a moment, then, to myself, answer: *I need purpose beyond myself and I need social contacts to avoid isolation. I also desire a certain amount of independence, my own autonomy, in which I am free to enjoy simple pleasures— the taste of good food, flowers, books, a walk in the sunlight and my need to write. I notice that I am less interested in the rewards of achieving and accumulating and more interested in the rewards of solitude and silence.*

Then, I wonder: How do we manage and accept limitations? I suppose the key word is "manage." And, because of the danger of losing what we have left, we are challenged to do the best with what we still have. Beyond the basic needs of comfort and safety, we want to enjoy life. We do not want to become disconnected from who we are or who we want to be.

As we age, the battle we face is the battle of maintaining control of our circumstances. We want to shape our own story. If we have an opportunity to do this, we will be fortunate, as shaping our own story is essential to sustaining a meaningful life.

I looked into the dark sky where the moon had been, then turned on the lights, poured another cup of coffee, paused, and realized again the powerful connection between living well and dying well.

In The Still Of The Night

I found I had less and less to say, until finally,
I became silent, and began to listen.
I discovered in the silence,
the voice of God

— *(Soren Kierkegaard)*

Phil and I were staying on the coast in a room overlooking the sea. In the middle of the night, I awakened to a full moon and a sky emblazoned with stars. Below me, the ocean was gently lapping against the rocks, and the large craggy cliffs loomed out over the coastline. I gazed through the glass door and quietly began humming the tune "In the Still of the Night"—you know the words: "In the still of the night, as I gaze through my window, with the moon up above and the stars in their splendor…" Then, that powerful question comes: "Do you love me as I love you?" And I stopped there, stepped out on the deck to a glorious still night and thought about the question. I was not thinking of my beloved husband, who was sleeping peacefully, I was thinking of our Creator God and felt I was being asked the question: "Do you love me as I love you?" And, if so, "Why don't you trust me more?" It was a love song with primordial sensuality. God loves us with a love that never lets us go. I know this; yet, do I love God enough to believe the question? It occurs to me that if we access the power of our senses, which so clearly connect the divine to our souls, we will find God in everything we do, there is no inner or outer to our spirituality. All that we believe will be of one piece, woven and worn together as one garment. Listening to the heartbeat of God, hearing God's voice, seeing God in all things and accepting God's love within creation, we recognize the world as a sanctuary and the whole of life as a sacrament. No matter what time of day or night or wherever we may find ourselves, we are assured of this everlasting love. To experience revelations of this kind in nature restores balance and quickens the imagination. I am grateful for this reassurance.

Autumn

A Season of Beauty and Necessary Decline

Summer and winter, and springtime and harvest,
Sun, moon, and stars in their courses above
Join with all nature in manifold witness
To Thy great faithfulness, mercy and love.

— *T. Chisholm*

Every year as the clocks turn back, I feel the ache of autumn. I cry out for the glories of summer and spring and the long days of light. My reverence for beautiful October tinges with melancholy as pumpkins disappear and bright orange colors fade into gold. All Saint's Day is observed and a sense of impending loss heightens to think of family and friends who are no longer with us. I search for certainty—hopeful ways to grasp this season of beauty and necessary decline—and ponder the mystery that living is hidden within dying.

Could it be that discernment of the spirit—this

relentless ache of uncertainty—comes to remind us that change and loss are a constant part of life? Surely this is a paradox we experience every autumn and eventually accept. Both light and dark are needed; like inhaling and exhaling, life requires both. How do we know what seedlings are planted within us during the dark nights of the soul?

To view the garden as metaphor is helpful. The roses will soon lie dormant, and as we shuffle through the fallen leaves and gaze at the stripped trees, we feel a kinship from our own losses, a stripping away. We ponder the season and notice a bright sadness mingling with our spirit. Nature's wisdom takes hold and with patience we acknowledge that the opposite of our uncertainty is faith.

Might we extoll the visual glories of this season and the hopeful notion that death possesses a beauty not seen. Autumn magnifies this testimony leading to the elegance of new life.

Advent Longing

My soul magnifies the Lord,
and my spirit rejoices…

— *From The Magnificat*

In the church courtyard stands a pristine marble statue of the Virgin Mary. Approximately four feet in height the finely featured face of the young woman radiates serenity. Her robes flow gently around her small body. Adding to her quiet beauty, I notice a shawl draped softly over her head and shoulders. What is different from other imitations are Mary's hands. Instead of being folded in prayer, they are dropped by her side with palms open— slightly raised above her hips. I meditate on this gentle posture and reflect on the moment Gabriel appeared announcing that Mary would bear the holy baby. I imagine the young woman's hands flipped, palms down, pushed out, and I hear her saying, "*Go away*, this is not something I want to hear. I am young and alone." Then she stops, ponders the message, listens and waits. Surrounded by a mysterious glowing light, Mary's faith is revealed. She opens her palms, lifts her hands and says, "Yes, let it be according to your will."

Later, she proclaims *The Magnificat:* "My soul doth magnify the Lord..., "followed by poetic words that compose one of the most beautiful passages in scripture. The young Mary, unafraid, with open hands and open heart, offers her message of acceptance, reverence and devotion. Poets and composers from Bach to Vivaldi have been inspired by *The Magnificat*—as are we. Throughout the season of lessons and carols, we listen, wait and long to participate in this sacred story.

Standing by the little statue, I contemplate the mystery and accept the divine gift of light we are given. Advent stirs within us and reminds us to nurture the light, grow in grace and wait in anticipation for the good news of re-birth, new insights and awakenings.

Akin to Mary carrying her child, we feel the spirit move, turn, and kick for our attention. Our souls are magnified by the grace we are given. We are not afraid to raise our hands, open our hearts and say:

"Yes, let it be according to your will."

Keep Ringing The Bells

Ring the bells that still can ring
forget your perfect offering
there is a crack in everything
that's how the light gets in.

— *Nathan Cohen*

When we confront confusion and ambiguity, accept our imperfections and brokenness, and dare not to get hung up on "if only," we begin to notice that it is through this "crack in everything" that the light comes in. We experience a new way of seeing—our perspective enlarges. We begin to realize that life on earth is not the place where we make things perfect—not our country, our world, our family, our work, our relationships, or where we live.

Very little, if anything, is perfect—even a rose has thorns and a new baby cries in the night. To acknowledge this reality, we relinquish our "white-knuckled" grip on life, live in the moment with our limitations and enjoy what we have left. As we learn to trust that all will be well, no matter, our spirit takes on new wings. The light we are given becomes a lamp for our feet and we are enabled to seek paths of hope and new awakenings.

Akin to this is the Christmas story. God imagined and created a perfect world, until it wasn't. Then, God cracked it open with the birth of the Christ Child and light came into the world. The child grew and from his powerful teachings we learn to keep ringing the bells of justice, kindness and mercy and radiate the light of faith, hope, compassion and love—and the greatest of these is love.

Confusion, ambiguity and imperfection are a part of life, and as we learn to ring the bells that still can ring, we dare to confront our challenges.

Let The Angels Sing

O Come, All Ye Faithful, Joyful and Triumphant

— John Franco Wade

Advent reminds us to listen for angels. They deliver important messages and we need to pay attention. The image of the angel Gabriel speaking to Mary poignantly speaks to us as well. His was a message she did not want to hear. In so many words, Mary said, "Go away," followed by "Yes, according to your will." We also hear messages from angels going to Bethlehem to view the manger and we imagine their angelic voices singing and filling the air, everywhere, with joy ringing through song. The carols of the season clearly reveal that our faith is a singing faith. Even though grief or pain is at hand, we allow our voices to rise with the angels and, with confidence, sing the familiar melodies echoing our praise and gratitude.

During a service of *Lessons and Carols,* I witnessed the healing power and joy of singing. On a cold, dark December night, our friends, Mary and Roger, accompanied Phil and me to a nearby chapel. As we made our way to a dimly lighted path leading to an elevator that lifted us to the chapel, I hoped we would not be disappointed as great effort was needed to maneuver our way through the crowd and to our seats. Our friend, Roger carefully led Mary, his wife of 68 years, with her walker. Mary was frail, weighed less than 100 pounds, and was totally blind. A poet and former writing teacher, Mary's life up to the time of her blindness was filled with books and literature. She read unceasingly until she could read no more. Her hearing, also impaired, distressed me and I wondered how much she would benefit from the service.

After we sat down, I noticed Mary bowed her head and waited. Then, the music began. As the organ resounded and the angelic choir burst into song, Mary's face brightened. Soon, the congregation joined the singing and as we went from one carol to another, Mary did not miss a beat. She remembered the words and sang with heart and soul. Don't ask me if she was in tune, I wasn't either, but together, with Phil in his wheelchair on one side and Roger on the other, we made a joyful noise.

At the close of the service, the organ boomed again with "Hark, the Herald Angels Sing" followed by "Joy to the World." My spirit lifted higher to see the glow in Mary's face and the wonder of a singing faith. At that moment, through music, her losses were transformed. This was Holy. This was Communion. The memory lingers like a holy whisper—perhaps an angel saying, "Yes, let it be, according to your will."

A Feet-Washing Experience

Forgive us our sins as we forgive
those who sin against us…

— *From The Lord's Prayer*

Our two-year-old granddaughter, Gloria, and her eight-year-old sister, Athena, came for an afternoon visit. Nestled in the family room the girls and their Grandpa Phil decided to watch an old *Mr. Rogers* film. Gloria crawled on Grandpa's lap and Athena sat on a nearby chair. Since the three of them appeared engaged and peaceful, I slipped away to another room and returned an important phone call. No sooner had I finished the call than Athena came running and said, "Grandma, Gloria needs you! She made a big mess in her underpants and is standing in it."

I heard Gloria whimpering and found her in a corner of the kitchen, quivering in her mess, feet and legs covered, trembling from shame and alarm. With no need to question, I picked her up, carried her to the bathtub, reached for the soap, and turned on the faucets. As the water washed over her soiled legs and feet, she lay limp in my arms, not saying a word. After the washing, I dried her soft little body with a warm towel, found some clean clothes and carried her back to the kitchen. She jumped down from my arms and ran to her Grandpa, crawled up on his lap and acted as if nothing had happened.

I returned to clean the bathroom, and reflected on the water from the faucet washing Gloria's tiny feet: How similar is God's love for us. We get ourselves into an unexplainable mess and are picked up, bathed in gentle love and made whole again. This act of kindness most often comes through others and we don't immediately recognize the divine power that has enabled the giver. Overcome with relief, we are also mystified and realize there is something more than a pleasant feeling of gratitude and joy, something deeper that stirs and awakens our spirit: God's gentle love has washed over us.

Throw Another Log On The Fire

At every turn in the road
a new illumining is needed
to find the way
and new kindling is needed
to follow the way

— John S. Donne

Grace arrived in its usual odd way: Weary of body and soul, I seek new inspiration and return to a favorite seaside inn where the air is fresh and the ocean comforting. I ask, *What next, Lord? Do you have something in mind for me?* What would happen if I drifted into some zone of idleness with no need of accomplishment or a feeling of being productive—just a blank page? How would it feel to be uncommitted, free of responsibility? My mind begins to imagine the future and a faint sadness envelopes me. I look out at the sea and ponder the endless horizon,

For distraction, I pick up a novel, find a comfortable chair in front of the wood-burning fireplace and strike a match to the paper wrapped around the stack of redwood logs. Within a few seconds, the fire blazes. I read a few chapters and then pause and notice the flames are slowly burning down and the logs turning to ash. Marking my page, I get up and throw new kindling on what is left of the smoldering logs. Sparks shoot up and the bright blaze returns. I throw on a heavier log to deepen the flame. Throughout the afternoon, I repeat the pattern. By evening, I am well into the novel but the wood-box is empty. *I must gather new kindling or the fire will go out,* I murmur, *Where do I go to get more wood?* Then, I remember: *the woodshed is around the corner, where it has always been. The endless supply of kindling and logs is stacked to the ceiling. How could I forget?*

My book falls on the chair. I run to the woodshed, fill my arms with kindling and logs, hurry back, and drop the load by the fireplace. As I toss the kindling on top of the dying embers, the flames again burst with light. I throw on one log after another until the blaze is restored and flaming.

The message is clear and I begin to pray: Gracious God, you speak to me through the fire. I know now that to keep burning, I depend on new kindling and fresh logs. Thank you for your endless supply. You do not intend for me to be a blank page. You intend for me to blaze with light and energy. Keep me mindful of your intentions and fully alive so I may glorify you forever.

The Wedding of Savannah And Elisha

Let the favor of the Lord… be upon us.

Psalm 90:17

I have been privileged to officiate at a number of weddings—each one vibrant with young people radiantly in love. In this collection of stories, I chose to include an excerpt from the following ceremony as this was an interracial marriage. Both the bride and groom were in the military. The family wanted the wedding a few days before Thanksgiving as the bride's brother and others were home for the holiday. The groom's family flew in from Alabama and as we all gathered at the Marin home of the bride's mother, it was apparent that the families did not know each other and I sensed obvious tension. After the ceremony and the eloquent, unscripted message offered by the groom's mother, what began as a "they and us" encounter developed into a united, inspired group who—with laughter and tears and expressions of gratitude—merged into one family. Did Elisha, akin to the prophet for whom he was named, perform a miracle? I wonder.

The Lord Be With You

Good friends and family, we come together
To honor the marriage of Savannah and Elisha,
to surround them with our prayers and grant
them our blessing.

From Psalm 90:17, we read:
Let the favor of the Lord our God rest
upon us, confirming what we do.
Thanks be to God for this amazing grace

As we reflect on the beauty of this
Thanksgiving season
this home and this gathering
we are mindful of the
beauty of God's presence and generosity
throughout all the complex events
leading to this sacred moment.
Because of God's precious providence,
each of us plays some part in this event.
Savannah and Elisha
want us here beside them tonight,
they want to say thank you for coming,
for believing in them
and to acknowledge that this ceremony
is not only a testimony of the devotion
they feel for one another
and the desire to be married,
but also an affirmation

of the power and mystery
of the Holy Spirit
as it is revealed to them

PLEASE PRAY WITH ME

Gracious God, always faithful in your love for us,
We rejoice in your presence and give you our
heartfelt thanks. You unite us as one human family.
You offer your tender words and lead us toward
the light. You open your loving arms and embrace us
with needed strength and courage.
We pray you will continue to assist Savannah and Elisha
with your grace. Fall afresh on their spirits
so with steadfast love and faithfulness
they may glorify you in their commitment to one another
and in the way they choose to live their lives.
And may the power of your Holy Spirit abide with them

✳ ✳ ✳

From the Gospel of John,
we hear these words of Jesus:
"As the father has loved me
So I have loved you.
Live on in my love
That my joy may be yours
And your joy may be complete."

HOMILY

Savannah and Elisha, before we proceed
with the vows, I want to speak
to our brief and meaningful moments together
last Saturday afternoon.
What you shared with me is
immensely telling in regard to who you are
and why you care so deeply for one another.

E.J., when we met, I didn't know your full name.
And, when you said, ELISHA,
my mind went to Elijah and Elias.
I drew a blank on the prophet Elisha.
Nevermind that I went to seminary, studied Hebrew
and am acquainted with the Hebrew Scriptures.
I could not recall the details surrounding the prophet's
life.
So, after you left, I went to the scriptures
and a few Bible commentaries
and renewed my knowledge of this mighty
and powerful prophet.
Let me tell you what I found:
As the immediate successor of Elijah,
Elisha inherited Elijah's wonder-working power.
And through the course of his lifetime
performed many miracles,
second in number only to Jesus.
He is especially remembered for his kindness
to those who followed him. Above all,

Elisha cared deeply about people.

This offers a mysterious footnote to our conversation.
One of the first remarks you made, Savannah,
in regard to E.J. and what you admire about him,
is that he gets along well with people,
and he cares about others, especially children.
Your family named you well, Elisha. And may the
Spirit of the great prophet abide with you tonight
and forevermore.

Also, Savannah, I asked,
"What is important to you in this relationship?"
You thought for a moment and then softly said,
"E.J. is just such a good man."

Then, E.J., I asked you,
"What is it you cherish the most about Savannah?
And you very simply and sincerely said,
"There is something about her
that is real that I have never found before."
In both of these responses,
I find sweetness and caring… caring
that goes beyond what we call a love relationship.
You both said you are never bored with each other,
and you enjoy each other's company.
You are good friends, and have often talked
about spending your life together, figuring things out
and taking care of each other.

It occurs to me that finding the right partner,
that person we want to come into our life and stay,
is a bit like panning for gold.
We dip into the stream of life
and a variety of options surface,
like attractive rocks of all sizes.
We sift and sort through them,
and a nugget of pure gold emerges into view.
I believe this is what happened to the two of you.
You were two athletes, you liked basketball
and you liked to compete,
you were an unlikely match.
Yet, you found something in one another,
something you wanted to hold on to.
And, it felt like gold.
I also asked you, Savannah,
"How do you feel about marriage and all that is ahead?"
You said, "The Gilberg women are strong women
and they have taught me to be strong."

A verse from Apostle Paul's letter
to the Philippians relates to this.
Paul talks about inner strength and the purpose
we each carry within. He writes: "God is at work in you,
both to will and to work his good pleasure."
All we must do is to believe in ourselves
and in the choices we make.
Tonight the two of you are given a sacred call
and asked for an awesome commitment.

You must vow to tend to your responsibilities
and to tend to one another.

The word "to tend" evokes an image
from my own childhood.
Remember, we are only two or three generations
away from pioneers and homesteaders
on this California coastal land
and upon the land
from which I came in Middle America.
And in some cases, only one generation.
As a child I was on the tail-end
of that second generation and lived
on a cattle ranch.
I recall what a great day it was when we exchanged
the old black wood-burning kitchen range
for a gleaming white bottle-gas stove.
This was before electricity came to the prairies.
Our new shiny gas stove had four burners and an oven.
No longer did we need to haul wood
and corncobs or carry out ashes.
All we had to do to keep the stove running
was to be certain the pilot light was burning.

Great attention was given to one raw flame
way down under the oven.
The old ranch houses at that time were drafty
and had very little insulation.
In the fall of the year, my father
would wrap black sheets of tar paper around

the foundation and bank the house with straw bales.
But no matter what he did, summer or winter,
drafts would blow through, and the draft
coming through the kitchen
would weaken or blow out the pilot light.
I remember my mother tending that vulnerable flame.
She would get down on her knees,
fan or blow on it, or strike a match,
then stand back and wait
until the flame started up again.

When you think a moment, isn't marriage like this?
A spark between two people grows into a flame.
Marriage is a choice to maintain the flame.
Savannah and Elisha, on this evening of your wedding,
may all that brought you together
and now burns like a flame within you,
withstand the drafts of discouragement, fear and despair.
May your dreams for your life together
fill you with abundant energy.
And, if the flame flickers or momentarily goes out,
I urge to go down on your knees,
strike the right match, and do whatever is necessary
to keep the burning.
May God's gracious love surround you
and the blessing of all of us here
abide with you now and always.

PRAYER AFTER VOWS

Let us pray: Gracious Spirit, faithful in your love for us,
hear our prayer and bless these spoken vows.
Fill Savannah and Elisha with light and hope.
Together may they fulfill a higher purpose
knowing that they are more than themselves
and more than each other.
May their marriage strengthen and sustain them
for the duties of life so that with steadfast love
they may honor the promises made this day
and be forever mindful of your love
|that will never let them go.

May the Peace of God be with us All. Amen

Memorial Service of John (Billy) Gross

My decision to include portions of a memorial service in this collection comes from my consideration that planning a service and delivering a eulogy is a privilege and I am deeply moved by doing so. Of the numerous ones I have written, none touches me as poignantly as the eulogy and prayers offered for the memorial service honoring Phil's younger brother, John (Billy) Gross, delivered July 9, 2011, in their home town of Freeman, South Dakota.

CALL TO WORSHIP

The Lord be with you,
Let us unite our hearts in prayer.

O God our help in ages past,
our hope for years to come,
we rejoice in the sure knowledge
of your presence and give thanks
for your tender mercies.

We come from many places and

through your amazing grace
we are bound together as one to form
this circle of love and remembrance.
We thank you for your blessing.

Hear our prayers—spoken and unspoken —
strengthen our spirits, fill us with hope
and peace so that when this hour is over,
we leave one another stronger and braver
for having been together.

As we recognize the wonders of life,
help us to accept the mystery of death,
trusting in your unfailing power
to grant life everlasting. Amen

A reading from Ecclesiastes 3:1-8.

EULOGY

Good friends and family, we come together to celebrate and honor John (Billy) Gross, to surround one another with comfort and share in the joy of a life well lived.

This is one of two services offered for John. The other, held at Fort Sam Houston, was distinguished with moving accounts of John's extraordinary military career. Today's service is distinguished because Billy has come home, home to Freeman, the town he revered. We gather as a community of love because, in God's precious providence, each of us has played some part in Billy's life.

Our memories reveal a variety of stories: childhood tales of chopping wood in Grandpa's back yard, running to the church on the corner, building model airplanes, picking apples from the family orchard, cleaning the cistern, fishing on the James River and hunting pheasants. Whatever he was doing, Billy displayed a sense of curiosity and enjoyed the people around him. He especially valued his childhood friends and kept them for a lifetime.

Although he traveled the world, the beauty of the South Dakota landscape never left Billy—the open sky and rolling farmland reflects the beauty of his generous spirit. He will be forever remembered for the twinkle in his eye, his hospitality, his sense of humor and his ability to forgive others and move on.

Then there was his flying. Just the other day, I saw a bumper sticker on a fancy car in San Francisco. It read, "Nice car, but I would rather be flying." I immediately thought of Billy as he much preferred planes over cars. Yet the mystery of his actual flying experience will never be known—we are left to acknowledge his acumen and to imagine his courage. We were proud of him.

As a young man the idea to fly caught Billy's imagination and never left him. He took pride in the planes he flew and drew respect and trust from those who flew with him.

The scripture reads: "There is a time for peace and time for war." Billy flew in the time of the Vietnam War. As much as we thought of him and wondered at his gallantry, we could not possibly know the danger he faced—day in and day out. The brave characteristics that made him who he was were revealed through what he did and his attitude in fulfilling his mission. Many of our questions about that season of his life remain unanswered.

What was it like to fly? The joy of buzzing Freeman, flying so low he would scatter chickens, stampede cattle and wave to farmers. And what of those times he flew over cities and crowds, in formation, wing to wing—like the day he flew over the service honoring John F. Kennedy.

What was it like to become one with an airplane to the point that it became an extension of himself—as with the F105, the plane he flew the most and so admired—a phenomenal machine extracting his total energy, precision and skill?

What was it like to fly one mission after another over North Vietnam—100 missions in all? What was it like to absorb the anxiety of taking off in the middle of the night and to experience the relief of returning?

The story of Billy's squadron, the Wild Weasels, known as the Daredevils of the Sky, is a story of courage, determination, dedication and perseverance—and it is Billy's story. What he and his fellow pilots were asked to do in the Vietnam War had never been asked of any pilots in any war up to that time. And what they did in taking out the surface-to-air missiles planted by the enemy was considered one of the most dangerous sorties of the war. The mere fact that the Weasel pilots accepted their command to take on missions deemed impossible is a testament to their bravery. Billy was one of those pilots.

As we know, many pilots were lost. And so we ask, what was it like to watch his buddies disappear in the night or to experience the long wait for planes that never returned? What was it like to complete those missions— especially the last two or three—wondering if he was really going to make it? And what was it like to come home from an unpopular war and live with the memories?

Billy seldom talked about the war. He seemingly let it go. Yet he carried a kind of emptiness that he could never dislodge. The evidence was there in his face and in his eyes. If he wondered about the mystery of human beings, with their staggering potential for both good and evil, he no doubt realized that the responsibility of being the judge who one day sorts it all out was not his responsibility.

Billy, or John, as he was known in the military, was a part of the history of the United States Air Force. He was given a job to do and he did it. He survived—and he left it at that.

From 14th chapter of the Gospel of John, we read:

Let not your hearts be troubled, believe in God,
believe also in me. In my Father's house

are many rooms, would I have told you
that I go to prepare a place for you, and when I go
and prepare a place for you, I will come again
and take you to myself,
that where I am, you may be also.

As I went over these verses, I thought this could also be the Gospel according to Billy. Can't you hear him saying, "Take it easy, don't worry, no sweat, I'm OK—there is plenty of room up here. I'm reunited with my buddies, and I'm waiting for you all to come and join me." He would likely add, "In the meantime, enjoy yourselves, don't be troubled, life is a great and wonderful adventure, and the only thing we know that we have for sure is right here and now. Don't miss it. I had a dream to fly—it was a bigger dream than I ever could have imagined. I learned how to attach myself to my dream, and live into it. I stood on the shoulders of a lot of people—many of you here today—especially Katie, Yvonne, Harvey and my childhood friends. You will never know the strength you gave me by just standing by and letting me go and do what I did best—fly.

And in the future when you think of me, I prefer you not think of me underground, but look up at the sky and know that I will be there flying in formation with all the great pilots who valued their country, their families, their friends and the town from which they came."

Amen

Music: "On Eagles' Wings."

Graveside Committal and Prayers
The Twenty-Third Psalm
The Lord's Prayer

BENEDICTION

Gracious God, ever present in the sunrise
and the nightfall, we thank you for unexpected
blessings. We see your fingerprints in Billy's life
and are grateful for the values and inspiration
he leaves with us. We thank you for the magnificent
sky he loved, the shining seas, the mountains
and the prairies, all valued during his life on earth.

May we go forth knowing that all is well with him
where nothing troubles, nothing frightens,
his mission on earth complete—Billy is home.

And now, may the God of hope and peace fill our hearts,
remembering always that we are loved with a love that
never lets us go. None of us lives alone and none of us
dies
alone. If we live, we live unto the Lord and if we die,
we die unto the Lord—so whether we live or whether
we die, we are the Lord's. Let us believe this to be
true—now and forever more.

Go in Peace.
Amen

Childhood Stories

We will not cease from our exploration

And the end of all our exploring

Will be to arrive where we started

And know the place for the first time.

— T. S. Eliot

This selection of stories is taken from my book, *Sunrise, Where It All Began* published in 2015. These childhood reflections from my life on the family farm use themes from *Alice In Wonderland*. The stories are dedicated to my grandchildren with the following sentiment taken from Lewis Carroll and his marvelous stories of Alice in mind:

* * *

"Afterward, she pictured herself a grown woman; and how she would keep, through all her riper years, the simple and loving heart of her childhood: and how she would gather about her other little children, and make their eyes bright and eager with many a strange tale, perhaps even with the dream of Wonderland of long ago… and how she would feel with all their simple sorrows, and find a pleasure in all their simple joys, remembering her own childhood, and the happy summer days."

— *Lewis Carroll, Alice in Wonderland*

Pa Young and The Small Town

"Either it brings tears to their eyes, or else –"
"Or else what?" said Alice, for the Knight had made a
sudden pause.
"Or else it doesn't, you know."

— *Lewis Carroll, Alice in Wonderland*

Our farm was located seven miles from the nearest small town of Wessington, South Dakata, population 300. Once or twice a week I would go with my parents to town where we bought groceries and needed supplies. Sometimes when Mother was grocery shopping Dad would take me with him to do other errands or to visit with the shopkeepers and town folk. I was seven years old at the time of my first encounter with Pa Young.

Pa Young owned the hardware/variety store. He was short, probably 5' 5" and chubby. His receding hairline left a shiny bald spot on the top of his head with a white fluffy rim of hair growing above and folding over his ears. With the exception of a small white mustache, he was clean-shaven and wore round glasses that slid down and pinched his nose. When he spoke and conversed with his customers, he looked over his glasses, which allowed his kind blue eyes to sparkle. A long-sleeved blue shirt was neatly tucked into his trousers, held by a pair of black suspenders. Everyone loved Pa Young. Not only was he generous but he often let customers take advantage of paying bills late or using a sliding scale in charging the country folks who frequented his store.

Dad knew I delighted in looking at all the variety of goods placed on the store counters and seemed to enjoy taking me with him. The store was small and my childish curiosity led me to the displays of kitchen towels, cups and glasses, salt and pepper shakers, scissors, needles, thread, knives, teapots and kettles. Everything was shiny and new, unlike our well-used utensils back home. As Dad talked with Pa Young, they could clearly see me roving around the store admiring and touching different pieces, but Pa Young always welcomed me and never seemed to mind my handling the merchandise.

Attached to the wall on each side of the store was a wide shelf, approximately four feet from the ceiling. This is where Pa Young displayed milk cans, galvanized bushel baskets and pails, horse collars and harness accoutrements, washboards, tubs, laundry baskets, butter churns, egg crates, fruit jars and canning equipment, and farm tools, including big circles of clothesline wire and bags of clothespins. On one of our trips to the store, I noticed a small square table with four chairs on the shelf. It was just my size and I was absolutely smitten. As Dad turned to leave, I ran to him and asked if we could possibly buy the table and chairs. He looked at me and sadly shook his head. The Great Depression was affecting everyone, but I wasn't thinking about hard economic times. I simply couldn't resist wanting what I was seeing.

Dad looked again at the little table and chairs and said, "How much is it, Pa?" Pa said, "Five dollars and 50 cents, but I will let you have it for $4.99." Dad said, "Joanie, I don't have the money right now, maybe later." As Dad scooped to pick me up and carry me out of the store, Pa Young motioned to me and said to my Dad, "Cort, wait a minute, I want to ask Joanie something." I slithered down from my Dad's arms and walked toward Pa Young. He said, "Joanie, I have an idea. If you will save 499 pennies, over however long it takes, I will save the table and chairs for you. They can stay on the shelf with a big 'SOLD' sign. How would you like that?" I looked at Dad and he said, "She will save the pennies."

Pa Young's offer must have circulated around the town as people began to give me pennies. First one and then another, including my Uncle Enoch, who owned the grocery store, and Mr. Light, who owned the creamery. They kept a little box by the cash register, just like we see today, and took out a few pennies every week for me. Our neighbors at the farm also saved pennies and the rural mail carrier occasionally left one or two in the mail box. I found pennies under my pillow and in my school lunch pail. Old Ed Gruber, our bachelor neighbor, even came one day and gave me five plus a Hershey bar.

I kept the pennies in a pickle jar and slowly saw the pile grow. When I went back to Pa Young's store, he would ask, "How many today, Joanie?" I would answer, "The jar is getting full, and it won't be long." Then, I would cast a long loving look at the shelf with the table and chairs. One day when I told him I had reached almost 400 pennies, he took the table and chairs off the shelf and let me look closer and touch them. The table was a honey color with three bears—a mama, papa and a baby bear— painted on top. The bears were sitting on a red and white checkered blanket. Pa Young signaled for me to sit in one of the chairs. I noticed how strong and solid the chair felt against my back and dreamed that one day I would sit for hours at the beautiful table.

Several more weeks passed and one day Dad said, "Joanie, have you counted the pennies?" I said, "I have 459." He then gave me a handful of pennies and filled my jar. Then he said, "How would you like to go see Pa Young?"

As we reached Pa Young's store, I saw him standing out front. I jumped from the car and ran up to him carrying my jar of pennies and joyfully shouted, "Pa Young, I have the 499 pennies!" He picked me up, swung me around in a circle, and then carried me toward the back of the store. I remember his jolly spirit as he carefully stood on the store ladder and handed the table and chairs down to my Dad. I gave Pa Young the penny jar and, without counting the pennies, he placed it by the cash register. As we said goodbye, I noticed him and Dad both wiping their eyes as if they were crying, but I couldn't stop to wonder, I was out the door, in the car sitting in the back seat with the table and three chairs and the fourth chair on my lap.

I kept the small table and chairs for over sixty years. Then, piece by piece they disappeared or fell apart. Decades have since come and gone, but the memory of Pa Young and my father wiping their eyes forever lingers. At the time, I could not understand why they would be so sad when I was so happy. Now, I do.

Milkin' Time

The Barn, Kittens, and Feeding The Calf

You're thinking about something,
and it makes you forget to talk.

— *Lewis Carroll, Alice in Wonderland*

I herded the milk cows through the wooded gate into the barn. Each one knew which stanchion to take and where to position herself for milking. On most summer afternoons, around five o'clock, I walked to the pasture to bring in the cows. Huddled together, they seemed to await my arrival. When I called, "Com-Bos, Com-Bos," their heads came up and their soft black eyes gazed calmly in my direction. Then, slowly, the lead cow started the walk toward the cow-path leading to the barn. Chewing their cuds and in no hurry, the five Holstein cows ambled along in a straight line with full pink udders slinging between their back legs.

There was freedom in going to the pasture alone. Every direction I looked, I discovered beauty and felt the spirit of nature. I was barefoot and loved to feel the tender, cool grasses of the pasture. The air was pure and refreshing and along with the immense sky and far horizon, my heart filled with wonder. As the evening breeze moved across the prairie, I stopped to pick a handful of wildflowers, watch butterflies, listen to grasshoppers and gaze at the sun lowering over the prairie. Because I wanted to take my time, I started early. The days were hot, temperatures in the nineties, and the cows smelled of milk, manure and sweat all mixed together. I grew accustomed to the smell as it was part of what went along with cows and I regarded all the farm animals as my friends.

Typical of most farms, the barn was dark red and faced the south to buffer the cold winter storms coming in from the north. There were several stalls built for horses and baby calves or an occasional sick animal. The stalls were musty gray and made from weathered lumber. A row of cow stanchions was built to fasten the necks of the milk cows in order to limit motion during milking. Beyond the stanchions and stalls, a wooden ladder was nailed to the north wall where we climbed up to the haymow. The hay was pitched up off the hay racks through the huge side door that dropped down from the haymow. The hay was used to feed animals throughout the winter months and also provided warmth and comfort to the barn. The loft was alive with birds flying in and out, mostly pigeons and barn swallows. Owls hooted at night and mice ran through the rafters. More than one mother cat gave birth to kittens in the hay. One year we had over fifteen kittens in the barn. I loved the haymow and often played there, making a house from the hay for the kittens. I pretended the kittens were my babies.

Most summer days were hot and dusty in the barn, and by evening, during milking, the air was intense and sticky from the sweat of the animals. There was also fresh manure from the cows which attracted hundreds of flies, darting and buzzing in every direction. My brothers cleaned the barn once a week, but it was hard to stay ahead of the pungent odor. The raw milk also had a pungent odor, but all this defined the barn and I didn't mind, as the environment was alive with activity.

My brother, Vince, milked three cows and my sister, Gladine, and I each milked one. My sister was good at many things but she hated milkin' time and found no joy in the barn. She would much rather be sewing with Mother or cooking. My brother milked the cows out of duty and was responsible for putting the milk in the milk cans and managing the cows. Neither my brother nor my sister understood why I liked milkin' time so much. But, I did.

After we washed the cow's udder with a rag and a pail of water, we picked up a milking stool. The stools were T-shaped and the trick was to keep our balance on the stool while holding the milk pail between our legs. The best way to do this was to lean our heads into the cow, then reach for the udder and hang on to the teats. This was the part Gladine dreaded as she did not want to get close to the

cow and often lost her balance and fell off her stool. I
liked to nestle my head near the cow's stomach and feel
the warmth from the hide. In spite of the rank smell and
the sweat, the cow's hide felt comfortable. To keep away
the flies, the cow would swish her tail. The tail was long
and hard like a rope until the last six inches where the hide
frayed out like the end of a whisk broom and never
stopped swinging. Moving through the air, the tail hit our
faces, backs and arms and kept the flies away, which was
a relief, even if dodging the tail was a challenge.

Once we settled on the stools, the milking began. My
brother liked to flip the teat from his cow and hit my sister.
His aim was perfect. He practiced by aiming at the cats
who stood about six feet away. The cats would open their
mouths and my brother would feed each of them with one
long squirt from the udder. Then, he would aim at my
sister. She would yell and stick out her tongue. My
brother would get a gleam in his eye and put his head back
in the cow's belly. I thought I could hear him snickering
and saying something to the cow. The cows didn't seem
to mind the fracas and kept on chewing their cuds and
swishing their tails.

When we started to milk it was noisy as the milk hit
the bottom of our pails, then, when the pails began to fill,
the sound would grow quieter and peaceful. After we
finished, my brother would take his pail and empty half of
it into another pail for the newly-weaned calf penned up
in a nearby stall. Then he would say to me, "Here, you
feed the calf." This was a delightful chore as baby calves

have beautiful soft eyes and silky coats. I would take the pail and fasten the handle around the calf's ears and stand back while the calf, with surprising strength, pulled and slurped. I marveled at the way the calf drank the whole pail of milk in one breath, then lifted his head, pail and all. I reached over and pulled the pail away. As the milky face came into view, I saw and heard the calf exhale and blow the milk from his nostrils. I loved that moment. I loved it all!

By the time the calf was fed and the kittens had all run to the haymow, my brother was moving the cows out through the barn door. "Shoo-Bos, Shoo- Bos," he quietly said. The cows walked a little faster now, stopped at the water tank and then slowly headed out toward the pasture. Milkin' time was over.

My Runaway Pet Lambs

Why, sometimes I've believed as many as six impossible things before breakfast.

— Lewis Carroll, Alice in Wonderland

In the Dakotas, lambing time usually comes in mid to late April after the sheep leave their winter shelters and roam the pasture. The sheep are quiet and hover together while the ewes drop their lambs. Occasionally, surprise winter storms blow through and, blinded by snow, the ewes are lost from the herd and often die giving birth alone. As a child, I recall sitting with my father on a tractor hitched to a farm wagon surging blindly across a field of blowing wet snow—looking for lost sheep. During one late April storm, when I was nine, my father and I found two orphaned twin lambs nearly buried in the snow. Dad said if I would feed and care for the orphans I could have them as pets. I was delighted.

After picking up the cold, wet baby lambs, I carried them to the wagon and jumped in beside them. I wrapped a grain sack over their trembling bodies and held them on my lap. As we bumped along back to the barn, I imagined how I would care for them and what names to choose. I knew it would be May or June before they were old enough to romp and play, so I decided to call them May and June. The lambs were white with black tails, black eyes and black noses. Very soon, they became my pets. Twice a day, from a tall brown bottle with a large rubber nipple snapped over the neck, I fed them cow's milk, cleaned their straw bed and filled the water trough. When I entered the barn, May and June would softly bleat, rub their curly hide against my legs and with their wet noses and soft tongues nibble oats from my hands. After they ate, I opened the barn door and led them outside to play. Before long, the lambs followed me all around the barnyard and bumped my legs for special attention.

A few days before July 4th, 1941, I announced to my family that I wanted to walk May and June in the annual parade. The summer celebration, filled with festivities for all ages, was held in our small town seven miles from the farm. By then, the lambs weighed nearly thirty pounds each and had coats of soft white furry wool. Often, I stroked my hand across their backs and nestled my nose into their sides. I thought they were quite beautiful and wanted to show them off.

World War II was imminent and the highlight of the small town commemoration was the patriotic parade with prancing horses, colorful bands, American Legion flags and serious World War I Veterans. Because I knew a few friends walking with dogs and kittens, and others riding ponies, I did not feel alone and was certain my lambs would blend well with the other entries. The first challenge was to figure out how to transport the lambs to the parade grounds. My older brothers, Bob and Vince, resisted the whole idea but my father consented. I was the apple of his eye and there was very little he would not let me do. At the time, we did not have a truck or small trailer. Our only choice was to haul the lambs in the backseat of our 1937 four-door Chevrolet. After a rope was tied around the neck of each lamb, Bob went on one side of the car with May and Vince went to the other side with June. They hoisted the lambs through the door into the backseat. I crawled on to the seat between my pets and held on to the ropes. Bob drove the car and Vince sat in the front passenger seat. My brothers were grumpy and, when out of earshot of my father, convinced me that this was "the dumbest idea they had ever heard" and I was going to ruin their 4th of July.

Bob drove me to the parade grounds near the town schoolhouse where we unloaded the lambs. He, then, turned around and drove back to the farm to get Mother, my older sister and Dad—handsome in his WWI uniform, leggings and all. Vince stayed with me and helped decorate May and June with red, white and blue crepe paper. Once he finished with the lambs, he wound the strips of paper around my arms and legs and placed a big dangling bow on top of my head (by this time, he was fed up and threw crepe paper in every direction). After securing a rope in each of my hands, Vince mumbled,

"Joanie, you better hang on darned tight." He then disappeared into the crowd.

I was given number seven in the parade lineup and nervously waited for the signal to move forward. At the sound of the bands warming up, the horses began to prance and May and June began to squirm. I admit to being a little frightened as the lambs tugged my arms, and my hands were already red and burning from the ropes. I kept thinking, *"As soon as we start to move, they will be fine."* I looked ahead and saw the Color Guard stand at attention and the town mayor in a car with a big sign: MAYOR HUTCHINSON. The pretty high school drum majorette lifted her baton, the drummer beat the big bass drum and the band members lifted their instruments to play John Phillip Souza's "Stars and Stripes Forever." The proud WWI veterans marched past me carrying guns on their shoulders. I saw Dad and was glad he made it on time. He winked at me as he passed, but did not move his head. (Bob told me later that he drove a speeding 60 miles an hour to allow Dad to be on time). After the horses and dogs, I was next and the parade began to move.

As the band played and the crowd cheered, I felt the ropes tighten and May and June started to run ahead and through the parade. Away we went, past the dogs, between the horses, alongside Dad and the straight-faced veterans, past the band and right through the middle of the Color Guard. My lambs and I were out ahead of the parade by fifty yards. Like a chariot with horses, May and June pulled me, and I could not rein them in—so I kept running. The town and country folks, waving flags on the street, looked surprised and amused, then began to cheer. I kept looking for my mother and brothers, but all the faces were a blur. We passed Chesbro Chevrolet Co. and the post office and headed for Main Street. I glanced at Uncle Enoch's grocery store, Mr. Light's creamery, the pool hall and finally the railroad tracks where, from out of nowhere, came my brothers. They did not say a word, just grabbed the ropes from my hands and stopped the lambs. Vince shook his head and led the lambs away. Bob, who always protected me, picked me up, put me on his shoulders, held my red burning hands and carried me down Main Street until we found Mother. I learned later that Vince led May and June to a stall filled with clean yellow straw in Harry Clark's big red barn. I was happy for them.

In spite of that dreadful experience, love for my pet lambs never wavered. What happened at the 4th of July parade was my fault, not theirs. We continued to play until I grew older and had other interests. I was not free to give them my constant attention. I imagined they waited for my face and touch to enter the barn door and wondered if I had abandoned them. What they could not know is that they were always in my heart and I would forever wonder at the mystery of our mutual affection, so full of light and love.

Playing Hide-and-Seek With Vern

Everything is funny, if you can laugh at it.

— *Lewis Carroll, Alice in Wonderland*

Vern, my childhood playmate, and I enjoyed the game of hide-and-seek. The environment was perfect as we had many places to hide and space to run. Devoted to the game and to each other, our hiding places were kept secret between us. We lived on family farms three miles from each other. Since we were the youngest children in our families, with no other boys or girls around except our older siblings, we often played together. The following story occurred when we were seven years old.

My mother, Martha, and Vern's mother, Adelaide, were friends and during harvest time worked together preserving vegetables and preparing meals for the threshing crews. Our fathers worked the machinery and shared ideas regarding farming, caring for livestock, and a wide range of politics. If one or the other were sick or fell behind with the field work, they helped each other or organized other farmers to lend a hand. During harvest time, the older siblings worked in the fields shocking grain. My older brother worked with my dad.

Since everyone was involved in the harvest, Vern and I were sent outside to play and no one paid much attention to what we did or where we were. We climbed haystacks, played with corncobs, chased chickens, mimicked hogs, teased cats, petted lambs, gathered eggs, picked wild flowers, and made houses out of grain shocks. Our favorite pastime was playing hide-and-seek. We played for hours; first I would hide, and then Vern would hide. The only place off limits was the windmill, considered dangerous because of the water tank—and we could not leave the farm yard.

One hot August day, as our mothers finished canning tomatoes in Adelaide's kitchen, Adelaide decided to make ice cream. No one could make ice cream like Adelaide and, on a hot summer day, nothing tasted more delicious. The eggs and cream came from the farm and ice was temporarily stored in sawdust. Vern and I ran to get our brothers and sisters from shocking oats and together we sat down on the front porch and ate ice cream. I loved to watch and listen as the tired families laughed and told stories from their hard day's work.

Vern quickly ate two bowls of ice cream, snapped his fingers to get my attention, whispered in my ear, and said, "Let's go hide." I recall Adelaide scolding him and telling him to stay out of trouble. I did not like her to scold him, but, on the other hand, Vern was mischievous—he loved to tease and he often misbehaved. My brothers used to say, "Adelaide scolds him too much—the more she scolds the more he looks for trouble."

My mother saw Vern take my hand and lead me away; she said, "Don't go far as we must go home soon." And we didn't. Vern led me into the garage, a few feet from the house, where we crawled under a pile of grain sacks. He arranged the sacks to allow air and light to come in. As we settled down to wait, we could see the house and the families sitting on the porch, but no one could see us.

After the ice cream dishes were picked up, washed and put away, my mother said it was time to go home as the cows were waiting to be milked, the eggs gathered and the chickens watered before dark. She also needed to fix supper for the men who were threshing in another field. Adelaide also had to get supper and work around the dozens of jars of canned tomatoes that filled her small kitchen. My mother told my brother and sister to "go find Joanie and get in the car." Vern's brother and sister went along to the farmyard and called our names. We were nowhere to be found. The four of them ran back to the house and said, "We have called and called and looked and looked and cannot find them." Of course, Vern and I were in earshot of all of this conversation, but Vern would not let me say a word. He put his hand over my mouth, pinched my leg and said, "Don't you dare answer, let them look awhile."

By this time, our mothers were frantic. Adelaide was crying and my mother was trying to keep calm. They were frightened and feared we had been kidnapped as recent reports of men escaping the State Penitentiary alerted the farmers to be on guard. The older boys were also sent to the water tank thinking we might have drowned. The more they called our names and cried, the more Vern giggled. I was scared and felt terrible, but did not want to betray my best friend. After all, it was just a game and Vern was having great fun. He enjoyed being holed up and hidden within a few feet of all "those big people who are always telling me what to do." Alas, he giggled once too often. His big brother, Howard, walked into the garage, heard the commotion and yelled, "Here they are." Both Howard and my brother Vince laughed and thought our game was a good joke, but not our mothers. They came running. My mother was sobbing. She picked me up with loving arms and said, "I am so thankful." Adelaide was not as loving. She said, "Vern, I know this was your idea, you come here." Mother gathered our family into the car and drove off. I looked over my shoulder, and out the window saw poor Vern with his pants down getting the paddling of his life. I cried all the way home. Mother and my sister never said a word, but I noticed my brother trying not to snicker.

EPILOGUE

At this writing, over seventy five years have passed. Vern and I have seen one another no more than a dozen times. Yet, when we do, we see each other as seven-year-olds and radiate inner joy that never leaves us. Vern still lives on the family farm. When I return for reunions with old friends, many who have lived on the same farm all their lives, Vern always comes and someone forever mentions our game of hide-and-seek. He tells me the old garage on his farm is still where it always was and he rebuilt the front porch where we ate ice cream. The windmill and water tank are gone as are most of the animals and stacks of corncobs where we played. We reminisce about our parents and how hard they worked; and we speak of the farm community, the many changes, and the freedom we had as children growing up on a family farm. As we leave each other, he looks at me every time, with the same twinkle in his eye, and says, "We really fooled 'em, didn't we?"

Duane

And the one-room country school

Which way you ought to go depends on
where you want to get to…

— *Lewis Carroll, Alice in Wonderland*

He came to our table, touched me on the shoulder and said, "Do you know who I am?" I said, "No, I don't, please sit down and tell me." Phil and I had walked into the Tailgate Café following my fiftieth high school class reunion held in Huron, South Dakota. The celebration honored my particular class but was open to anyone who had graduated from Wessington high school—a small town thirty miles from Huron. After the festivities, most of my classmates went on to another party but, weary from our travels, Phil and I opted to take a walk. We came across the cowboy café and thinking the local color might be interesting, we went in for a bite to eat. As we sat down, I noticed, toward the back of the café, a table of men about our age, but because I lived away for so many years, I did not expect to recognize anyone.

The stranger was tall, lean and ruggedly handsome. He wore a brown western style shirt and pants, cowboy boots, a bowler tie and a silver belt buckle. His grayish brown hair was combed straight back, enhancing his strong featured face and penetrating blue eyes. Without speaking, he reached his hand out to Phil, pulled up a chair and sat next to me. For what seemed like a long time, he only looked at me with a warm gaze. Finally, he cleared his throat and said, "I never thought I would see you again. I am Duane. You and I went to grade school together." I said, "How did you know me?" "My younger brother, Claire, was at the reunion and told me you were in town. When you walked through the door of the café, Claire nudged me."

Suddenly the years melted away. I was a little girl in a one-room country schoolhouse, a long way from anywhere. Under a big sky and an endless horizon, the white clapboard one-room school stood alone in the corner of an open field. In the back and in opposite corners of the large playground, not far from the small horse barn, were the two wooden outhouses—one for the girls and one for the boys.

The door to the schoolhouse was on the south. Beyond the door was a small entry way where we left our overshoes and wet or dirty clothing. As we came into the large room, we turned left to a cloak room where we put our lunch pails, extra clothing and supplies. Our teacher, Mrs. Ford, carried water daily to fill a large earthen stoneware water jar with one tin cup attached to the rim. The earthen jar sat on a small table in the corner of the room. During the winter months, Mrs. Ford also stoked the coal burning stove in the basement. In the large room, there was a chalkboard on the east wall and a bank of windows on the north wall. Above the chalk board hung a portrait of George Washington. The American flag stood on a pole in the corner. The wooden desks with wrought iron legs faced the east. Mrs. Ford summoned us to classes by ringing a handheld brass bell with a black wooden handle. Because all eight grades were together, some desks were larger than others. The desk top fascinated me as it opened and shut. I stored my pencils, eraser and books beneath the wooden cover and loved knowing the space underneath, and all that was in it, was mine. This was my world, everything else in school was held in common. I attended this one-room school seven years and for most of that time, depending on the year, I was the only girl with eight to ten boys.

The farm families lived within three or four miles from the schoolhouse. Most of the school children rode horses, carried their lunch in tin syrup pails, put the horses in the school barn, fed them a handful of oats at noon and rode home after school.

Mrs. Ford taught all eight grades and created a memorable environment. As the older children helped the younger children, we learned from one another and a feeling of intimacy prevailed. Later, I realized how the common classroom offered a unique educational process.

Although we were isolated, we were taught respect for our country and our farm community. What we learned related to building character, good citizenship and practicality. In the morning we stood in a circle around the flag pole and took turns raising the flag, then gave the pledge of allegiance. At the end of the school day, we formed the circle again, lowered and folded the flag and carefully handed it to our teacher. During recess we ran and played on the school yard, games like "Pump Pump Pull Away," "Kick The Can," "Ring around The Rosie," "Anti I Over," plus hours of Kitten Ball. The only playground equipment was a Teeter Totter which my Dad made from two barrels and a long board. We loved the Teeter Totter and took turns riding up and down for hours on end. Besides balance, we learned that in order to have a smooth ride we had to watch out for one another so as not to hit the ground suddenly after jumping, or get off at the bottom and let our partner fall and be injured. We helped each other have a good ride. Of all the lessons learned from that handmade Teeter Tooter was the realization that we could not ride alone.

School was a happy place as we discovered a freedom not always possible in many of our homes, especially for the boys whose fathers depended on them for farm work. World War II was in process and times were harsh. Frustrated by drought and depression and far too much to do, many fathers were ruthless in the work they demanded of their sons and only allowed them to go through eighth grade. Often the boys carried scars of abuse. They learned to deal with menacing prairie winters—relentless freezing conditions—alongside extreme domestic circumstances. The schoolhouse became a safe space—a comfort zone. Fathers were desperate and mothers often sick from overwork and isolation. Some of the stories cling to my memory like barnacles to the bottom of a boat. It has taken many years for me to see this part of my life as a source of wisdom and an occasion for poetry. The schoolboys were rough and tough, they had to be, but they, like my brothers, were very good to me.

All this flashed through my mind when I heard Duane's words, "We went to grade school together." Through the years, I kept up with a few of the boys and because my name was in the local paper announcing that I would be attending the reunion, several had come to welcome me home. But I lost track of Duane and only remembered that he had not gone to high school as his father demanded he stay on the farm and work. Most of the farmers knew Duane's father was an abusive man and hard on his three boys. Duane was the oldest and suffered the most. Even if neighbors and Mrs. Ford were aware, little attempt was made, at that time, to interfere in domestic problems. My mother reached out to Marie, Duane's mother, as she knew Marie was worn and weary from years of sadness. Our pleasant one-room school offered a safe place and Mrs. Ford was gentle and treated us with tender regard. She encouraged us to care for one another. I was a year older than Duane and after graduation from eighth grade, I did not return to the country school and never saw or heard of him again until our surprise encounter at the Tailgate Café.

After we chatted about the usual questions of where we lived, our families, work, etcetera, Duane started to reminisce about life on the farm. He told us that one day, when he was sixteen years old, he saw a plane fly over the farm—an uncommon sight on the Northern Plains in the early forties. He looked at the plane and decided to leave home. He walked away from his threatening father, hitchhiked to the nearest town, and joined the Air Force. He enjoyed a successful military career and life was good. He spoke of his wife as a "fine woman." They had been married 45 years and now lived in Kansas. Duane had come back to the family farm to visit his brother.

Later, we shared stories of days in the one-room school house. The ponies in the barn, the games we played and our wonderful teacher. Speaking of the barn evoked memories of Eddy, who could ride a horse like no one else. He was fun and a great chum to all of us. Duane smiled as he recalled the day Eddy and I were running and I fell over Eddy's feet. My face hit my dinner pail and I broke out my two front teeth. The other schoolmates came running and heard me ask Eddy, "Is there anything wrong with my mouth?" Eddy replied, "No, I can't see anything." I told Duane that I had repeated the story at the reunion earlier that evening and Eddy, who was in the audience, stood up laughing and said, "Joanie. you asked me if there was anything wrong with your mouth, you didn't say anything about your teeth."

After a few more stories, Duane fell silent. I was struck by the amazing intimacy between us and grateful as Duane was filling in missing pieces of my own childhood story. Then he touched my arm and said, "Before I go, I want you to know that you were important to us in that one-room country school. We cared about you. We were a bunch of rough neck boys, you were this girl in our midst, someone soft and kind and feminine. We wanted to take care of you. Personally, you gave me hope. I had no sisters and my mother was sick and overworked. You were the only girl I knew and I have never forgotten you."

As Duane stood up to leave, once again his face flushed with emotion. He steadied himself with one hand on the table, touched Phil's shoulder with the other, looked him in the eye and said, "You take care of that girl." As he walked out the door with his brother, he turned once more and waved. Phil looked at me and his eyes flooded with tears.

Jug Brown And My Dog, Pepper

Alice: "How long is forever?
White Rabbit: "Sometimes just one second."

— *Lewis Carroll, Alice in Wonderland*

Among my many farm pets, including lambs, a one-legged duck and my pony, I had a favorite little dog, Pepper. He was short haired, slick black with two white back paws. Above his beady eyes and pointed nose stood his short ears, always erect. He was small and weighed about ten pounds.

Pepper was more like a toy as I carried him under my arm, somewhat to protect him from the bigger farm animals. I also dressed him in doll clothes and pushed him around in my doll buggy. He would lie perfectly still on his back or sit up, but never left the buggy. He was supposed to sleep in a little bed on the front porch as Mother did not allow dogs or cats in the house. This was the custom among the farm women during those dusty days of the Great Depression. They believed there was enough dirt coming in through the window sills and dirty farm clothes without adding more from domestic pets.

We had larger dogs as well. I remember their names: Sandy, Spotty, Ace, but I did not consider them to be pets. They were on the farm to send out barking alarms to strangers who came or to scare off predators—wolves, coyotes, weasels—that would sneak in at night and kill lambs, baby calves or chickens. I remember Sandy being killed one dark night by a wolf that entered the barnyard to drag off sheep. My father heard the commotion too late for Sandy, but he shot the wolf and the lambs were saved. We buried Sandy by the barn and I made a small cross to mark his grave.

These big dogs were called "sheep dogs." They were loyal and fierce, but not my pets. For the most part, Pepper and I stayed clear of them, even if I was grateful for their protective manners. Their eyes followed us wherever we wandered. The big dogs could hear and track most all the wild animals except the weasels. One night over a dozen laying hens were killed by a weasel that entered the chicken house while the dogs slept nearby. Weasels are small animals with brown fur and thin bodies. They are sly, very quiet and able to wiggle through small holes or cracks in the foundation of a building, like a chicken house. A weasel is a nasty predator, especially with chickens. My parents put up chicken wire and did everything they could to protect the laying hens, plus keeping the dogs at hand, but that particular evening, the weasel slipped by and caused great havoc in the chicken house. After that, my father set traps and, to protect them from the traps, tied up the dogs. Eventually, the weasels died or were afraid to come.

While it is true that Mother scolded me for bringing a dog into the house, she was fully aware that I sneaked Pepper into my bedroom at night, even if I thought she didn't hear me. Later, I realized she knew how much I loved him and thought I needed a playmate as my brothers and sister were older than I. At bedtime, Mother would come to my room, knock on the door without coming in and simply say, "Sleep well, Joanie." By this time, Pepper was in bed, sleeping on his back with his four paws folded on top of his little body. My bedroom was near a door leading to the front yard and I would get up early and let him out to run, thinking Mother didn't know. Later, I realized she did.

One late summer afternoon, about dusk, and shortly before supper, Pepper and I were sitting on the porch step near the front yard. I heard a loud rumble and a faint jingle, and then noticed a cloud of dust on the road in front of the house. Jug Brown, driving his Mobil Oil fuel truck, was making his last stop of the day to deliver gasoline. Jug was a big man with big hands smeared with grease. He wore overalls, a dark jacket and a black cap snugly placed on his round head. His rugged face was weathered and he smelled like gasoline. The dusty red truck carried a large tank of fuel with a log chain dragging on the ground. The chain was suspended from the rear axle to the ground to dissipate the electric charge—avoiding sparks—to prevent the truck from catching on fire and causing an explosion. Because of the late hour, Jug Brown was traveling rather fast as he turned into the driveway. With darkness looming and the dust swirling, I could barely see the truck, but I heard the dangling chain jingle. Focusing on the chain, my arms must have loosened as Pepper suddenly jumped away from me and ran toward the truck. I screamed his name but my voice did not carry over the noise from the truck. He ran directly in front of the big wheels. Jug Brown saw me running and pulled the rig to a stop, but not before the truck had run over my little dog.

He opened the door and jumped out just as I reached down to pick up Pepper, who lay lifeless on the ground. I carried him in my arms and ran toward the wind-mill and the water tank saying, "I will give him some water." I was aware that Jug Brown was running behind me. I kept saying, "He is OK, isn't he, Mr. Brown?" There was no answer. Then, I said again, "The water has to help him, don't you think?" Still no answer. As I looked at Pepper with disbelief, so quiet and still in my arms, I said, "You ran over him, Mr. Brown, Pepper did not understand your big truck." My arms tightened around Pepper and I felt cold and numb. It was then that I heard the loud sobs coming from behind me. Jug Brown was crying and could not speak. He took Pepper and laid him on the ground and then put his arms around me, picked me up and carried me toward the house. He never stopped sobbing. He looked at my dad and mother and mumbled, "I'm so sorry, I will come back tomorrow." He walked quietly to the big red truck, turned around and slowly drove away.

Through the years, Jug Brown continued to deliver our fuel and drove carefully as he entered the driveway. He and my dad were good friends and I often heard Dad reassuring him that I was OK. Yet, when he saw me, even in the small town where we did our shopping on Saturday nights, he would always seek me out and quietly put his arm around me.

Time moved on and soon I was in high school. Jug Brown's son, Lyle (we called Jughead), was in my class. He was a friend and knew the story of his dad and Pepper, but we never talked about it until our 50th high school class reunion. After not seeing me in fifty years, he came up to me and said, "You know, Jo, Dad is gone now, but he never stopped hurting from the fact that he ran over your little dog." I looked at him, paused, and said, "And I never stopped hearing him cry."

My Pony, Jack Slater and My Dad

Everything's got a moral, if only you can find it.

— Lewis Carroll, Alice in Wonderland

Within an eight-mile radius of our farm lived a community of twelve families. With the exception of Jack Slater, who was known to be unfriendly, we were a convivial and robust group of folks.

Jack lived three miles from us and supplemented farming by operating an ice house. In subzero winter weather, he chopped ice from a nearby pond, trimmed the chunks into approximately fifteen inch square blocks and carried them to the icehouse, a dark barn with no windows. From floor to ceiling, using a large grasping claw-like tongs, Jack stacked the blocks in sawdust. The owner of the local lumber yard, in exchange for ice, gave him the sawdust, which Jack shoveled into his truck and unloaded with a bushel basket. Without electricity, the farm homes depended on ice for refrigeration. The square block was purchased and placed in the kitchen icebox, a square cupboard with a lid that lifted up to allow the ice block to be dropped in and cool the cupboard below.

The milk cows provided plenty of cream and during the hot summer, we often went for ice to make ice cream. On Sunday afternoons, neighbors gathered under shade trees in our farm grove for an ice cream social. Each family brought a freezer of prepared cream. Dad provided the salt and bought the ice from Jack's icehouse. He carried the chunks in gunny sacks and, with the back of an axe, the men chopped the ice blocks into small pieces. Everyone took a turn at the crank. When the ice cream was frozen and the dasher removed, the children came with spoons for the first taste. Since there were several flavors, we were nearly full by the time the actual serving began.

Jack Slater sold a lot of ice those days but never came to the parties. His wife, Mae, died several years before I knew him. They had no children. There were those who said Jack was the cause of her death, others said he was mean and not to be trusted. The farm women were afraid of him and would not go alone to the icehouse. Some men were also wary as Jack carried a pistol and kept an ornery-looking dog.

The one neighbor who could talk to Jack for any length of time was my dad, who felt sorry for him and his bitter existence. When Dad went for ice, he took a pint of whiskey and he also took me. I was eight years old and Dad was proud of my singing voice and thought Jack would like to hear me sing. Even though Jack, with his piercing black eyes, raspy voice, dirty clothes and unshaven face, was scary to me, I looked forward to our trips to the icehouse. It was something my dad and I did together. Between the whiskey and my childhood songs, Jack and Dad would visit. They told stories and Dad could make Jack laugh.

I was fascinated with the huge tongs used to pick up the ice blocks and the sawdust on the floor. While Dad and Jack talked, I entered the icehouse and pretended it was a castle. Breathing the distinctive damp, musty odor, I climbed into the spaces where ice had been removed and imagined I was a princess. Dad and Jack stood at the open door and a dim light came through, which allowed me to see the stacks of ice as I ran freely among them. When we were ready to leave, Jack would cry and Dad would slap him on the back and say, "It's okay, Jack, we will come back soon and Joanie will sing some more."

One visit, Jack showed us his new car, a two-door white Ford. Most farmers drove black cars, but Jack chose to be different. The other neighbors gossiped. They may have been jealous, as in those frugal years the new Ford car was swishy and novel. Dad believed Jack craved attention and this was one way of getting it.

In November 1940 the snows came early. One morning, as I rode my black Shetland pony, Tippy, to the one-room school house, the snow banks were especially high and the wind was blowing. I rode without a saddle and carried my tin lunch pail in my right hand as I held onto the reins with my left. For miles, no matter which way I looked, all I could see was snow. The grayish-white sky hovered like a blanket over the white land. Since Dad had bridled the pony and tied the reins together and Tippy knew the two-mile ride to school, all I had to do was sit on his back and ride.

Suddenly, like a ghost, Jack Slater's white car emerged in front of us. Tippy reared and threw me to the ground, with my foot tangled in the reins. Then, he started to run back toward the farm, dragging me behind him. Jack Slater jumped out of his car, but it was too late. Tippy was a quarter-mile down the road. Because of my winter clothing, I did not feel anything except the ice and snow under me. I was not afraid, but Jack later told my dad that he was "scared as hell." He moved the white car as close as he dared to Tippy and eventually grabbed the reins. The frightened pony, snorting through his frozen white whiskers, eyes ablaze, finally stopped. Jack took off the bridle, hit Tippy on the rump and sent him down the road toward the farm. Then he came over to me, picked me up, held me very close and said, "Are you okay?" He asked if I wanted to go back to school or home. I said, "I want to go to school." Jack turned his white car around in the middle of the road and took me to school. Then he drove away to find my dad.

A few years later, the Rural Electrical Association brought electricity to the farms. The government program meant we had an electric pump for running water, indoor plumbing and refrigeration. There was no more need for the icehouse. Jack Slater was out of business. Rumors continued and people were still afraid of him. The talk was that he kept women. Dad never believed the rumors and continued his visits. I did not see Jack again. I was growing up, going to high school and on to college. My days on the farm were over.

Thirty-three years later, married with three children and living several hours away, I made a sad trip back to visit Dad, who had suffered a stroke and was spending his last days in the town hospital. He could not speak. As I sat beside him, every hour the hospital room filled with visitors. I knew many of them, but one day, while Dad and I were alone, a man appeared at the door and I could not recognize him. I nodded and the stranger walked slowly into the room, toward the bed. He looked at Dad, then at me, hesitated, and started to cry. After a few moments, he turned to me and, in a very low raspy voice, said, "You are Joanie, aren't you? I'm so glad you didn't get hurt." I knew it was Jack Slater. He touched Dad's hand, looked once more at me, wiped his eyes on his shirtsleeve, and quietly walked out the door.

We March and We Sing

Mrs. Lorensen and the Young Citizens League

Always speak the truth, think before you speak,
And write it down afterwards.

— *Lewis Carroll, Alice in Wonderland*

I am often asked when and where I learned public speaking and singing. My quick and correct answer is "In the One-Room Country School." With eight grades in a single room, there had to be a high degree of structure and discipline, but with the flexibility of personal attention as well. To that end: drill, recitation and memorization were the basic ingredients for learning. From first grade on, I recited poems and readings in front of the other students. Performance at this age had a profound effect on me and before long my teacher entered me in a number of school district and county contests. Often, I would both sing and recite readings. My parents also coached and encouraged me and, as time went along, located a retired teacher who gave me private "public speaking" lessons.

No doubt, my most profound influence came from performance opportunities provided through The Young Citizens League (Y.C.L.), an organization popular in the era of one-room country schools. The school-based club had the goal of improving citizenship and character education. At one time, the national organization had an estimated 75,000 members in 4000 chapters.

The Hand County chapter (where we lived) was organized by a remarkable woman, Winifred Lorensen, County Superintendent of Schools. Mrs. Lorensen visited our school twice a year and I will never forget her. A stout woman in a black suit and a crown of beautiful silver-gray hair, who quietly entered our school room and left an indelible impression. To reach us, she drove a small black car over many miles and through all kinds of weather and road conditions. Welcomed by our teacher for encouragement and necessary corrections, she also brought inspiring new ideas. One of her main objectives was to promote participation in the Y.C.L. She took us by the hand and insisted that we enter the district speaking contests, as well as art, poetry, and musical competitions. A wise educator, Mrs. Lorensen knew that, along with thousands of children like ourselves, the Y.C.L. would give voice to those of us who learned in rural one-room isolation. She offered opportunity for us to share our talents with others and promoted our rhetoric and unashamed idealism concerning God, country and family. She also taught the memorable Y.C.L. Marching Song. At the close of each school visit, we students would move the desks to the middle of the room; form a line behind our teacher, who carried the flag, and Mrs. Lorensen. Then, we marched in a circle singing the Y.C.L. song at the top of our voices.

Mrs. Lorensen noticed my natural speaking talent and encouraged Mrs. Ford, our teacher, to enter me in the regional contests. I was in the third grade and for the next five years I entered many contests and unabashedly won first place in all of them. My mother was embarrassed when another mother, rather sarcastically, said to her, "I see no point in entering my daughter in a contest where Joanie is speaking—she wins them all." I honestly did not think too much about winning as I practiced for hours and loved to speak. My greatest pleasure came in pleasing Mrs. Lorensen who presided over the contests and, as she handed me the blue ribbon, put her arm around me and said, "You did well, Joanie."

In the spring of my eighth grade year, the state Y.C.L. convention was held in Pierre, the South Dakota state capital. Mrs. Lorensen asked if I would be the toastmistress for the banquet, which would be held in the large hotel next to the Capitol building. She explained that I would introduce the governor and other dignitaries and present a brief essay on what Y.C.L. had meant to me. Approximately 300 people, including teachers and school delegates, were expected to attend. My parents were also invited. They were ecstatic, albeit a bit apprehensive. Even though they were talented leaders in our small community, nothing like this had ever happened to our family. They did everything possible to prepare me for the occasion. I remember my dress, which I am certain, for us, was expensive. The skirt was brown velvet and the top a turquoise knit. I loved it. Mother fixed my hair and Dad made certain I had white stockings and new black patent leather shoes. My brothers and sister gave me a great send off. I don't recall being anxious, only excited and curious.

Mrs. Lorensen requested I arrive early in Pierre and come directly to her room, which was in the same hotel as the dinner. She said she would accompany me to my seat at the banquet and introduce me to the delegates. I planned to meet Mother and Dad at the conclusion of the evening.

In the hotel room, Mrs. Lorensen quietly coached me as to protocol and gave me a list of names in the order I would make the introductions and asked that I lead in singing the Y.C.L. Marching Song. She told me where to stand for my remarks and what I might say to Governor Sharp. Then, she tenderly took my arms and massaged a fragrant hand lotion up and down each arm. I remember the aroma of the lotion and the comfort of her gentle touch. After she finished, she took my hands, placed them in my lap and softly said, "You will do fine, Joanie, I am proud of you."

THE Y.C.L. MARCHING SONG
We march and we sing; our voices ring;
Young citizens are we;
Leagued in a host whose watch-words are

Youth, courage, loyalty.
Hailing our nation's banner,
Afloat in the sunlit sky,
Which through hopes and fears,
through future years,
We will hold evermore on high.

My Grandmother and The Sunshine Party

She tried to fancy what the flame of a candle looks like
after the candle is blown out

— *Lewis Carroll, Alice in Wonderland*

I grew up singing and reciting readings for the Sunshine Party, held at the Community Church every September beginning in 1931. Inspired by my grandmother, Hattie Hutchinson, who imagined the event as "a mission to gather the elderly and provide an afternoon of entertainment and refreshments," the party, after eighty-five years, continues to thrive. With the exception of the name change given to the Ladies Aid, who host it, and the church basement transformed into a new fellowship hall, the venue of music, readings, and food and fellowship remains—often with the great-great-granddaughters of the original women presiding.

Organized in 1883, the Community Church was located in the small Central South Dakota town of Wessington, population 300. The church served both town and country—the farm families living within an approximately ten-mile radius. Although there was a Catholic church on the edge of town, the Community Church was the largest and, in 1931, had around 175 members. Predominately of Celtic origin, the families originally migrated to the eastern states and eventually moved westward with families, finding farm land and building small towns on the Northern Plains. The town and farming community was alive with activity. Festival days were celebrated and a good spirit united town and country. Albeit loosely organized, the church was the center of worship and, along with the school, dance pavilion, local businesses, post office and pool hall, blended into the fabric of community life. The congregation loved to sing as did the intergenerational choir (I started singing with the adults at age eleven). There were many potluck suppers, basket socials, talent shows and participation in the Saturday night community hall dances. The "preachers" were respected but not necessarily revered. They came from different denominations and did not adhere to the creed of any particular church. The hard-working people were an independent lot and the ministers did not stay long. In the mid-nineteen-forties, the church was reorganized and became under the aegis of the Presbyterian Church.

In the summer of 1931, known for her typical Scots-Irish feisty manner, Grandma Hutchinson confronted the church pastor and said, "All you think about is your sermons and what you will say at funerals. Don't you think it is about time we did something to honor our older members and friends in the community?" The pastor, a younger man, backed away, then replied, "What would you suggest, Mrs. Hutchinson?" "Well," Grandma said, "Many of our older members are not able to socialize; they are lonely and need company. I would like to have a party and bring all of them together at one time." "You go right ahead, Mrs. Hutchinson, perhaps the ladies of the church will help with expenses. You have my blessing." "Well, I should think you would come and at least show interest, maybe say a prayer or something. These older folks are the backbone of this church and community and some of them will still be here after you are gone." The young pastor nodded his head. He knew better than to confront Hattie Hutchinson.

Grandma Hutchinson called on her friends who swiftly made a list of the older members and other elderly people in the community and set a date for the first party in September. Their dream was to make it a joy-filled day and all agreed with Grandma's suggestion for the name. From then on, "The Sunshine Party" became a household word, if not an institution in the small town. The first party was held in the basement of the church, where receptions and social gatherings took place. There were tables with pretty napkins, flowers and tablecloths. Music and readings were performed and time allowed for favorite hymn requests. The model was set and became a tradition.

I was five years old when I recited my first reading, and either spoke or sang at every party until I graduated from high school. Other young people also performed and a few of us sang duets and tap-danced. We often read the poetry of Edgar A. Guest, a favorite of the time. The older people enjoyed patriotic songs, such as "You're a Grand Old Flag," and sang along. The program was not complete until we sang "You Are My Sunshine."

When I started high school, my friends and I also helped with serving. This was a wonderful opportunity to be with elders, even if we found ourselves being silly, as teens will typically be. I remember one party when Mrs. Huestis wanted only hot water to drink, but with milk. That prompted us to giggle, and then Mrs. Harris had trouble getting out of her chair. As two of us tried to help, we slipped and nearly pulled the dear soul to the floor. Mrs. Coop was too large for an ordinary chair, so we had to find one that fit her size. Mrs. Major, very deaf, kept jumping up and down with excitement, and Mrs. Wedge and Mrs. White just sat and smiled.

Tea sandwiches, cookies and cakes were donated from town and country. I remember the soft white bread with ham salad and the aroma of egg coffee boiling in large pots. Mrs. Prentice usually supervised the kitchen. She was a big strong farm woman known for her chickens and eggs and she always made dozens of deviled eggs. My mother was known for her beautiful angel food cakes and came with three or four. They were known as the "specialty of the house." Several women brought sunflowers and other garden bouquets. The old basement rocked with vibrant color and hospitality.

When I was about twelve, the memory that lingers is the sound of voices raised in singing the old hymns. The requests came so quickly that Mary Chesbro, at the well-used upright piano, could barely keep pace and she pounded the keyboard with such vigor that the flower bouquet on top waved precariously back and forth. Grandma started with *Lead, Kindly Light,* followed by *Abide with Me,* and *In the Sweet Bye and Bye.* Mrs. Bottom called for *Let the Lower Lights Keep Burning* and *Sweet Hour of Prayer.* Mrs. Hazzard requested *In The Garden* and *Rock of Ages.* After *I Love To Tell The Story,* Mrs. Peddicord rose from her chair, stood tall and straight, hair pulled tight in a twist (she owned the local beauty parlor) and said, "I want us all to march and sing *Onward Christian Soldiers.*" There was a scurry of motion and effort, but everyone stood and began to march in place, one foot and then another. Some of the feet could barely lift, but the sound of shuffling and singing filled the room. The minister arrived in time for the marching and Grandma, with raised eyebrows, asked him to pray. She then lifted her arms and said, "We will now close by singing *God Be With You Till We Meet Again.*" The refrain—"till we me-ee-eet, till we me-eet"—was repeated more than once and I noticed eyes filling with tears. At the time, I did not know why. Now I do.

Thanksgiving
Our Favorite Family Holiday

I wonder if the snow loves the fields,
that it kisses them so gently?
And then it covers them up snug, you know,
with a white quilt;
and perhaps it says,
"Go to sleep, darlings, till the summer comes again"

— Lewis Carroll, Alice in Wonderland

There are numerous reasons why our family loved Thanksgiving. Mother and Dad were relaxed and happy as the harvest was over, the corn picked, hay stacked, garden produce preserved, butchering finished, and the house banked with straw bales to keep the floors warm during winter. For the feast, nearly all the food prepared for our Thanksgiving table came from our own bounty, including the lard for the pumpkin pie crust and the whipping cream.

Preparations for the Day began early: relatives invited, chairs counted, tablecloths washed and ironed, dishes organized, and finally the cooking began. Mother made pumpkin pies, corn pudding, sweet potatoes with marshmallows, dinner rolls and dressing for the turkey. Then, she cooked potatoes for mashing, green beans and stewed tomatoes. Later, she would make the gravy. More food would come with the relatives. Nothing, however, compared to the drama involved in fattening, dispatching and preparing the huge turkey.

Early in autumn, near the granary, Dad built a woven wire pen, approximately five by six feet. The pen was tightly secured with a woven wire roof and strong stakes to hold the fence on the sides. From our flock of 20 - 25 domestic turkeys, Dad picked out a strong tom turkey, placed him in the pen, and the process of fattening the Thanksgiving turkey began. Every day Dad tossed shelled corn and silage into the pen and filled the water pan. Sometimes, he let me toss the corn.

I found myself going often to the pen and loved watching the big turkey eat, grow fatter, and strut around with his huge fan-like tail. Dad warned me not to get too attached. But, I did, and dreaded the day the turkey would become the centerpiece of our Thanksgiving dinner.

Dad took seriously his responsibility to dispatch the turkey in the least cruel way. Proud of his marksmanship, his plan was to aim his rifle at the big bird's head and kill the turkey with one shot. Dad was a hunter and, to him, accurate handling of a gun was great sport. From the trenches of World War I, he knew how to shoot. He was also a native of Tennessee and grew up within a few miles of Sergeant Alvin York, a war hero. Sergeant York learned his marksmanship from shooting wild turkeys in the Tennessee hills. During the war, he led a small band of American soldiers against an army of several hundred German soldiers and won the battle, largely because he instructed his men to come up behind the enemy and shoot from the back in the manner in which he had learned to shoot wild turkeys in Tennessee. As a teenage boy before he left Tennessee, Dad had known Alvin York and loved to tell the story of the hero who was his idol, especially as a gamesman. So, two days before Thanksgiving, Dad took his rifle and went out to the pen alone to kill the bird. The family stayed in the house and waited to hear the one shot. Dad never missed, and the turkey never suffered. Difficult as it was for me to think of the turkey being killed, I couldn't help but be happy for Dad when he walked back to the house and said to Mother, "I did it with one shot, Mam."

Once the turkey was scalded in a big tub of boiling water and the feathers removed, one of my brothers carried the bird, usually weighing between twenty-five and thirty pounds, into the house for final preparations. After the giblets were removed, Mother took over with the task of removing the pinfeathers. I often helped her as this was time-consuming and Mother was very particular about removing every feather. She would then wash and dry the bird and put it in a cool place overnight. On the day before Thanksgiving, the turkey was placed in a roasting pan and the cavity filled with mounds of bread, celery and onion dressing. Mother would then melt a pan of home-churned butter and pour it over the bird. There was enormous excitement as the big white bird was lifted into the oven of the wood-burning kitchen stove where it would cook all night. Dad would stoke the firebox before he went to bed and, I imagine, checked it throughout the night. By morning, the house was filled with the aroma of roasting turkey.

By 11:00 on Thanksgiving Day the aunts, uncles, and cousins had all arrived. The men sat in the living room and discussed crops, grain storage and politics while the women cut pies and assembled more food in the kitchen. At 1:00 we gathered around our long dining room table. Mother usually gave the blessing and others would read or share thoughts of gratitude. The bounty of food was served and passed "family style." Positioned at the end of the table was the brown-buttered roasted turkey. After the prayer of thanksgiving, Dad picked up the large kitchen knife and carved the big beautiful bird.

Since we only used our cream for whipping on holidays, there was more excitement when it came time for pumpkin pie. The cream was whipped with a hand beater and did not take long as the fresh cream was thick, tasted divine, and could almost be eaten without whipping. We children were excused from the table to help with the whipped cream and looked forward to licking the beaters. After dessert, the men usually took a nap and the women did the dishes. We children went outside to play. If the snows had come, we went sledding; otherwise we played in the haymow.

While it may be true that the Thanksgiving meal demanded the greatest attention, there was no doubt but what those who gathered came with thankful hearts. As farmers, we celebrated what the land provided and gave thanks that the hard work of plowing, sowing and reaping was finished for the year. In The Dakotas, we knew that the winter storms would soon begin and long cold days awaited us. On Thanksgiving Day, however, no one spoke of what was coming; what mattered was what the harvest had yielded and what was safely gathered in. Farmers, around our table, felt the just reward of their labor. Hearts were lifted in praise and gratitude. It was a holy time, a time to rejoice and celebrate.

Prairie Flowers and Wild Turkey Eggs

Where and What Formed My Spirituality

I know who I was when I got up this morning,
but I must have changed several times since then.

— *Lewis Carroll, Alice in Wonderland*

To breathe is to pray. This knowing began in childhood. My people were honest, hardworking farmers and neighbors with an emphasis on community life. As a family, our belief system was integrated with the spirituality of the land; we had few conventional religious rituals. Mother, however, made certain we attended the community church and from age seven on, I recited readings and sang in community programs. The hymns and caring concern for one another within the church family deeply touched me. While I don't recall an emphasis on teaching, I recognized a moral compass at work within our culture. We learned right from wrong and good from bad, and we nurtured respect for the dignity of others.   Neighbors were to be trusted and business dealings were closed with a hardy hand shake.

As the youngest of four children, I walked and played alone. Solitary time with the land and the animals, under a big sky with an endless horizon, shaped my consciousness and formed my spirituality. I enjoyed watching the horses run in open fields and felt sad when they were harnessed and made to conform. I understood why cattle and sheep broke fences and wondered why gates were necessary. I fed and cared for orphaned lambs, herded milk cows, gathered eggs, played with dogs and kittens and rode my pony. The beauty of sunrise and sunset, prairie flowers, wild turkey eggs, butterflies and chokecherry jam captivated me.

From this environment, my life in the spirit began. I experienced a strong residing force within me, a force that watched over me while I ran and played, and cared and comforted my doubts and fears. I felt loved with a love that never let me go. From this came a radiant inner joy. I learned to converse with this inner spirit. Later, I realized I was learning to pray and find grace in all that happens.

Except for the following incident, I don't recall any specific occurrence that shaped my spiritual development. At the age of five, Mother took me to a Pentecostal Vacation Bible School held in a small country church three miles from home. Several children my age attended. I remember being asked, "Those of you who would like Jesus to enter your heart, raise your hand." I raised my hand, even though I only vaguely knew who the teacher was talking about. I recall how I felt at the time: My arm went straight up and I said "yes" to something or someone that day. I remember thinking about my heart as a special place deep within me. This was my first glimpse of an inner sanctuary and refuge, a home to which I would forever return.

During the years that followed, I realized the value of my childhood experiences. From them, a vision unfolded...a vision that would lead me to higher purpose and stay with me throughout my life.

338

Afterword

Now that I have collected these essays and stories, I realize that without a significant amount of idealism together with outright realism, I would not have had the courage to write them. By idealism, I mean my belief that behind the challenges of being human there exists a divine realm of meaning that defines us and grants us purpose for our lives. By realism, I mean a desire for my writings to feel authentic, both sophisticated and simple—because they are.

Through imagination and art—that is, a way of expressing myself—I am inspired to keep the central element in my work filled with light. Accompanied by goodness and mercy, I use light as a way of shaping attitudes and intentions within the stories and essays I write.

My greatest regret is that I could not name and write about every particular person who has given meaning to my life, because I find a story in each one and I have known many wonderful people. How I would love to bring them all together, including those in this collection. I imagine a long table wrapped around the world at which we are all sitting and engaged with one another. There are friends from cities, country-sides, several nations and a variety of cultures—a remarkable portion of humanity. And if strangers drop by, they will be welcome. On top of a white banquet tablecloth with napkins there are bouquets of flowers everywhere. There is music and I see low glowing candles. I imagine the guests blowing kisses and celebrating the moment. And I see them giving thanks for all that has been and all that shall be.

Holy is the thought.

About the Author

Jo Vaughn Gross grew up in Central South Dakota. She is a graduate of the University of South Dakota and the San Francisco Theological Seminary. She was the Founding Director of The Banquet, a model feeding ministry to the poor and disadvantaged, in Sioux Falls, South Dakota, where she lived and worked with her husband,

Dr. H. Phil Gross, an orthopedic surgeon. Jo is published in the *Journal of Pastoral Care.* She is the author of *The Welcome Table,* a primer outlining her method and intent of feeding the poor with dignity and respect. Her collection of childhood stories, *Sunrise,* describes her experience of growing up on a family farm. She lives in Northern California near her children and grandchildren.

Made in the USA
Middletown, DE
15 September 2018